5.95

D1094259

Champagne Tony's Golf Tips

Champagne Tony's Golf Tips

by Tony Lema with Bud Harvey

McGraw-Hill Book Company

New York   Toronto   London

Contents

1

The beginning of the beginning

A Wee Drop o' History

Nobody seems to know just how or when the game of golf originated. Or, for that matter, even why. As far as the antiquarians are concerned, the game apparently was handed down to us out of the Dark Ages along with thumbscrews, tight collars and other tests of virtue and humility.

The Hollanders filed a patent claim on the strength of some old Delft tiles which picture a group of burghers whacking away at a small object with curved clubs. But the scene is clearly wintry and the action is taking place on ice, presumably a frozen canal. It looks more like a scrimmage between the Boston Bruins and the Detroit Red Wings than a rehearsal for the Ryder Cup matches.

The Dutch support their claim with old manuscripts that identify this form of ice hockey with the words "kolf" and "kolven," meaning "club." The phonetic similarity between "kolf" and "golf" is supposed to clinch it.

Actually, I suppose the first slice in history was played by some Assyrian shepherd boy who got tired of counting mutton and took a swipe at a stone with his crook. But it remained for some unsung Scots shepherd to bore a couple of target holes on the barren moor, substitute a more resilient object for the stone—perhaps a crudely rounded block of wood—and utter the first "Oh, dom!" over a missed putt.

Things have never been the same since.

Much later, some creative genius invented the "feathery." This primitive golf ball was constructed with three pieces of leather—two polar caps and a broad equatorial belt—stitched together to form a sphere. A small opening was left, and through this hole the ball maker stuffed "one tall hatfull" of freshly boiled chicken feathers, and the hole was closed. As they dried, the moist feathers expanded to fill their leather jacket and the finished ball was painted white.

The feathery ball had all the playing qualities of a wad of bubble gum, but it was an improvement. After you've been hammering a chunk of boxwood across the dunes, anything is an improvement. The demand for featheries far outstripped the limited production facilities of the day. A good ball maker, minding his own business and staying away from the pub, could turn out two or three feathery balls a day. And there was a lot of production down time. It seems many of the ball makers contracted a sickness, believed to stem from handling the chicken feathers.

Meanwhile, the original shepherd's crook with its gnarled head was slowly evolving into a more sophisticated hand-hewn tool. Carefully selected tree limbs were shaped and scraped to form broad-faced clubs with varying degrees of loft. They looked more like field hockey sticks than golf clubs, as we know them. But their fifteenth-century users didn't care. They called them all "spoons" anyway—long spoons, middle spoons and short spoons.

As a matter of fact, they *looked* like spoons. The faces of these early golf clubs were spoon-shaped. That is, they were concave, or scooped out. It wasn't until somewhere along in the late 1800s that an Englishman named Henry Lamb went the other route and decided to make himself a set of woods with *bulging,* or convex, faces. Oddly, it was discovered that these convex club faces, while tending to exaggerate a natural slice or hook, actually improved the player's control over the flight of the ball. But this developed only after the clubs had been in play long enough to have the daily pounding flatten out the bulge. With this astonishing discovery, all the club makers abandoned the traditional spoon-shaped wood and, ever since, these clubs have been manufactured with a slightly convex, or perfectly straight, face.

Funny thing, shortly after I won the British Open championship, I contracted to endorse a practice gadget that embodied the principle of the old-time spoons. Picture, if you can, a plastic tee peg surmounted by a plastic bowl large enough to hold a golf ball. Now, cut away the front half of the bowl and you have a practice tee which cups the ball on the back and on both sides. The idea was that, using this crutch, the chronic hooker and slicer could forget his troubles and enjoy the thrill of long straight drives. I dunno . . .

The iron club has been with us a long time. But it was conceived originally as sort of an all-purpose trouble club, great for digging the old featheries out of cart ruts and sheep tracks. There really wasn't much point in developing it for anything else. You couldn't very well belt the old feathery with it or you'd flatten out the ball like a pizza.

Actually, in the days of the feathery, another club—the first small-headed wood—was designed for the same kind of work. It was called a wooden niblick and was used to rout the ball out of tough lies. Because it saw a lot of hard use, the sole of this niblick tended to become scarred by contact with rocks, frozen turf and roots. Someone thought to screw a brass plate on it and it came to be known as a "brassie," direct antecedent of the No. 2 fairway wood.

Meanwhile, however, Scots by the hundreds were deserting their sheep crofts to manufacture feathery golf balls and smuggle the game across the border into England where it became rather fashionable. The first golf course in England was built in 1608 at Blackheath and consisted of five holes. In those days there was no standard number of holes on a golf course. Prestwick, in Scotland, had twelve. St. Andrews started with six and eventually grew to eighteen. The first eighteen-hole course ever built was Westward Ho! in Devon, England, and the reason it was laid out as eighteen holes was because the builder was Tom Morris of St. Andrews who simply took the St. Andrews links for his standard. Thereafter, by common consent, eighteen holes became fixed as the standard length.

The game already had survived one crisis. An early Stuart king called off all matches and sent everyone back to the archery butts for instruction in the use of the longbow. He was scared to death the French might sneak across the Channel in the black of the night and catch every able-bodied Britisher on the back side.

Subsequently, an audit of the palace books turned up an interesting item, an expenditure for "golfe balles and clubbes," and the jig was up. Everyone had a good laugh at the Crown's expense, and rushed off to the links for a fast nine holes before dark. Trying to stop the evolution of golf with a royal edict was like trying to stop a cattle stampede with a traffic light.

As a matter of fact, in 1642 another Stuart king, Charles I, was lining up a 12-foot putt when a messenger brought him news of the Irish Rebellion. He missed the putt.

And Seumas Graham, Lord Montrose, who led the Scottish clans in their last stand against the English, shared the Stuart zest for the game. Legend has it that he tore himself away from the course to get married and, a few hours later, was back again for another round.

Actually, the early fears of King James were realized, though. The French *did* arrive. But they were carrying golf clubs. When James' kinswoman, Mary of Scotland, took up residence at the palace, it turned out she hadn't been spending all her time at the harpsichord while she was stashed away in France. She had picked up the golf habit, too, and she introduced the first caddie—or "cadet," as she called him in her Parisian brogue.

And so we derive the caddie, a club-bearing biped which became extinct during the early years of the Golf Cart Age. It's a pity, too. Out of the caddie pens came a half century of America's greatest golfers, including the Sarazens and the Hagens, the Nelsons and the Hogans. Yes, and so did that chap, Lema. The passing of the caddie marked the passing of the true *golf professional,* as distinguished from the *professional golfer* who simply plays golf for money.

But we aren't particularly concerned here with the rise and fall of the golf "cadet." Our interest lies in the snapshot history of the game, and more specifically, with the very recent development of vastly improved playing equipment and how it has influenced the fine art of hitting a golf ball. So, let's hurry along.

The gutta-percha ball, or "guttie," came along about the time the Sioux dog soldiers were bushwhacking the first wagon trains somewhere west of Fort Laramie. The guttie ran into a lot of stormy opposition, not the least of it arising from the entrenched ball makers who saw the new product stealing their morning porridge. But, the truth is, the guttie came along in time to save the game which, in the early years of the nineteenth century, had declined sharply in popularity in Scotland. The guttie, selling for about one-fourth the price of the feathery, brought the game down to the pocketbook level of the tradesman.

But it took quite a period of trial and error, and sulphuric controversy, before the guttie ball received the grudging approval of Scotland's dour old arbiters of golfing fashion. Its acceptance opened the door for the introduction of the iron-faced club. Now golfers had a ball they could flail with an iron blade without fear of flattening it out like a poultice.

Experiment proved that "dimpling," or scuffing, the surface of the guttie eliminated an early objection: that the guttie ducked and side-slipped like a wounded goose. Roughing up the surface gave the ball "claws" for grabbing the air, enabling it to hold a true flight trajectory. So, with good distance, reasonable accuracy and an attractive price tag, the new ball was a cinch to drive the feathery off the market and usher in the Iron Age of golf.

The guttie split the golfing *aficionados* into two factions —those who accepted a machine-hammered ball and those who insisted on hand-hammering. Right up to the dawn of the twentieth century there were die-hard Tories who insisted on hand-hammered guttie balls, arguing that hand-hammering hardened them.

For a while, the Eclipse ball threatened to eclipse the popularity of the guttie. It was made of softer material and had the special virtue of retaining or returning to its round shape better than the guttie. Also, it held its line better on the putting green. But it was a heavier ball, size for size, than the guttie and lacked its carry. Further, it shed its coat of paint quite readily when in play. What with one thing and another, the wave of popularity for the Eclipse washed itself out almost as quickly as it rose.

The rubber-core ball, marking the arrival of the modern game, didn't appear on the golf professional's shop counter until after the turn of the century. Francis Ouimet tells a poignant story of his first experience with the rubber-center Haskell, which he retrieved from a water hazard at The Country Club. Hoping to dry it out, he slipped it in with his mother's baking bread. Some time later, the family's attention was attracted to the kitchen where the aroma of baking bread was heavily spiced with something considerably more pungent. Pulling out the bread pans, Francis found his precious ball—the cover burst and simmering in its own juice, the interior a writhing snake pit of bubbling elastic!

The golf ball was standardized in 1921 by edict of the Royal and Ancient Society, which fixed a weight of 1.62 ounces and a diameter of 1.62 inches. Eleven years later, the United States Golf Association adopted a somewhat larger ball (1.68 inches in diameter) of the same weight.

But it's the evolution of the golf club, from the crude wooden bludgeon used to beat the feathery into submission, that raised the fine art of hitting a golf ball to the realm of a pseudo science . . .

I know there are many, and especially on the other side of the great Atlantic water hazard, who will contend that the word should be "reduced" rather than "raised." They regard the American golfer as a steel-shafted robot who plays the same damn shot from tee to green—then putts out and goes on to the next hole, where he re-sets his stroking mechanism and repeats the same dreary mechanical process all over again.

Well, they won't get any argument from me. Everyone is entitled to his cherished prejudices and I'll go along with George Bernard Shaw, whose response to this type of challenge was always a quiet, "You *may* be right." It didn't mean he agreed with you. He was just motioning for you to play through.

The early golfers, and they were good ones, got along nicely with very few clubs. Even after the guttie ball made hand-forged iron heads practical and popular, the daily bag limit at such playgrounds as St. Andrews and Prestwick and Musselburgh was about seven clubs. In 1860, the red-jacketed gentry at these three Scottish clubs got together and put up a belt, emblematic of the British Open championship. Ten years later, young Tom Morris of St. Andrews won it for the fourth time hand-running and retired it, carrying only six clubs—two woods, three irons and a putter. And he shot the tough Prestwick course in 74–73!

Along about this time, the shortest of the woods—called the "baffy"—was being superseded by an approaching, or lofting, iron. Tommy Morris had a special genius for this shot and this contributed materially to the growing popularity of the club. Morris also was quite handy with a niblick that was designed originally for getting the ball up out of a bad lie. However, it was felt that the face of this club was too small for the ordinary player to use it accurately and so a club called the "mashie iron" was introduced—sort of a compromise between the niblick and the lofting iron.

This was the age of experimentation in golf club design. The club heads were shrunk to bulldog size on the theory that, by reducing the size of the large "spoon" heads, the full weight of the clubhead could be massed directly behind the point of contact with the ball. The iron putter came along to replace the wooden one and a "driving mashie" appeared—actually just a short-headed cleek.

As recently as 1900, the average golfer carried an assortment of not more than seven clubs. These included a couple of woods (a driver and a brassie—or a cleek), a driving mashie or driving iron for a running approach, a mashie for lofted approach, a niblick for bunker play and a putter. The baffy was obsolete but still used by some who couldn't master the approaching irons. The "dynamiter" appeared on the scene about now, for extracting the ball out of sand.

These iron heads were riveted to wooden shafts, usually hickory because of its toughness and spring. For the wooden heads, beech and sour apple were commonly used. Later, persimmon became popular for its great resilience and fine grain.

Golf "sticks" in this period were a heterogeneous collection of cats and dogs, purchased and replaced individually. A guy needed a mashie, so he went down to the club maker's and bought himself one. Perhaps he tried four or five, discarding each one in a burst of irritation, until he found the one that felt just right. Matched sets were matched in name only.

Andra Kirkaldy, the old Scots professional, is generally credited with developing the theory that the lighter club produced a longer drive, basing his argument on the thesis that the speed of the clubhead is the critical factor when striking the ball. From this stemmed a period of experimentation to determine a suitable clubhead weight to impart a sufficient blow. Wooden shafts had a degree of "play" in them, including a torsion factor, that made striking a golf ball truly an art in those days. Each shaft had its own individual combination of spring and torque which required some adjustment by the player as he became familiar with the club and confident in its use.

So we move along into the stately Edwardian Age. With only a handful of misfit clubs at his command, the serious golfer of the Gaslight Era had to master a wide variety of shots, ranging through a whole spectrum of changing conditions. There was the full shot and the half shot, the soft and choke shots—and, of course, that endless source of aggravation, the flubbed shot . . . followed invariably by a few more shots at the 19th hole to help him forget.

It was a time when the caustic observer of the sporting scene could write with absolute justification that golf was a game "in which a small round object is propelled about the landscape with a set of tools poorly adapted to the job."

As we have seen, this was true as recently as the early 1900s when Ouimet was still caddying in Brookline, Massachusetts, and the august United States Golf Association was 50 yards short of puberty. With a magnificent sense of fitness, some legendary Scottish preacher called golf "the 'umblin' game" and put his finger on its great natural appeal.

There's a little of the flagellant in all of us and I think we like to punish ourselves as penance for some real or imaginary sins. Golf is a wonderful outlet for this overpowering sense of guilt. Christian, slogging through the Slough of Despond, is a happy wanderer compared with the poor devil lining up for his third charge at a ball buried under the lip of a bunker.

But even the most guilt-ridden doesn't want to spend his entire life in the stocks. We all like to prevail over our torments. And so, mastery of the mashie-iron became an obsession with the country club gentry, and the outcry for golf instruction brought swarms of canny Scotsmen to these shores, each with a firm conviction that he alone held the secret key to unlock the mysteries of the golf swing.

From the outset, golf in the United States was identified as a game reserved for the upper crust of society. This was because, by its very nature, it was restricted to the country clubs. To purchase and develop 200 acres of land close to a population center required an impressive investment to begin with, requiring in turn the patronage of wealthy captains of industry to underwrite the project. For them and their families, there was a need for a massive and costly clubhouse since, in the main, they were more concerned with personal comforts and status than in the game of golf.

Thus, from the beginning, the American golf installation represented a sharp departure from the British prototype, which was Spartan in its simplicity. It grew and flowered in a social enclave, well isolated from the mainstream of American life.

But when Ouimet knocked off the two British titans, Vardon and Ray, at Brookline in 1913, the golf virus escaped from the laboratory and infected the entire American body politic. Capitalizing on the popularity explosion of the game in the United States, the Thomas Wilson company, manufacturers of sports equipment, reached across the sea and borrowed former British amateur champion P. A. Vaile's catechism of instruction, *Modern Golf,* and began reprinting it, chapter by chapter. Thus was begun the first American five-foot shelf of golf instruction, a piece of furniture that has required constant and energetic carpentry ever since to keep pace with the cumulative writings on this fascinating subject.

The Americans, with a characteristic zest for fun and games, swarmed into golf. Stimulated by Ouimet's stunning upset, they had to defer taking direct action until the world's difficulties with Kaiser Wilhelm could be settled. Then, swept along on the crest of a great postwar prosperity wave, the American people rushed into the Roaring Twenties waving their Scottish insignia: a bottle of bootleg hooch in one hand and a Forgan mashie in the other. Golf, which Ouimet already had made socially acceptable on the wrong side of the tracks, became a status symbol with ultimate sanction by the broker, the banker and the candlestick maker.

Many Irons in the Fire

What followed was inevitable. With tens of thousands of Americans screaming for golf "sticks," the American genius for mass production was challenged. There weren't enough Willies and Jocks in the world to keep up with the demand for artfully hand-crafted golf clubs. In the early 1930s, America's new Beau Sabreur of the links, Bobby Jones, conceived the idea of producing a matched set of clubs. In the history of the game it can be compared to the day the physicists fractured the atom under the football stands at the University of Chicago. The matched clubs, identical in balance and swing weight, could produce matched shots. And soon the tool shops began turning out first steel shafts, then fully matched sets of woods and irons.

Suddenly, almost overnight, those familiar old friends, the hickory-shafted mashie and the warped old spoon, wound up hanging in glassed wall cases. In their place was a dazzling set of matched irons, a group of faceless strangers numbered from 1 to 9, and a new triumvirate of shining wooden faces answering to such noncommittal names as 1, 2 and 3. Later were added their more slope-shouldered brethren, 4 and 5.

But the new breed of "sticks" had the redeeming virtue of uniformity. Right down the line, they responded unerringly to the call of duty. Unvarying in manufacture and interchangeable in play, the matched woods and irons at least gave the American golfer what he wanted, according to Henry Longhurst, the delightfully urbane British golf writer—the opportunity to produce a "standardized golf stroke with your standardized set of clubs."

Americans, said Henry, like to play what he calls "target golf."

"They like a good lie, a flat stance, no wind, every mechanical aid in the shape of the newest super-super something-or-other shaft; and then see with what precision they are able to 'shoot.'"

I think Mr. Longhurst was showing the thin edge of acerbity when he penned those lines, but you can't deny that he was playing around with something that has elements of an eternal verity. The American, even when relaxed and at play, doesn't have much patience with uncontrollable factors—or even those difficult to control. He likes to eliminate all the delicate filigree and get right down to the basic contest: my golf stroke against yours. It's a national weakness, or strength, depending on your point of view. In any event, I think Henry has a point. I wish him well with it.

Back now to the Ugly American. His disorderly passion for order was satisfied when he could lay in a supply of matched woods and matched irons, handsomely bagged in a portmanteau large enough to carry the caddie. Now he could study the Table of Standard Distances and begin to maneuver this troublesome game into a corner where he could pounce on it and wrestle it into submission.

Here is a table, showing the average distances for both men and women that can be expected of each club, with its degree of loft. A student of the game will commit this table to memory and, later, will establish a matching set of club distances to measure his own game. This is Lesson No. 1 in "target golf," to borrow the Longhurstian phrase.

Many professionals today don't carry the No. 2 wood (the old brassie) or the No. 1 iron (the driving iron). They prefer to carry the 4 as the third wood and, of course, the wedge is indispensable today. No. 10 and No. 11 irons are rarer than dodo birds. Forget about them. I know a few pros who carry the No. 1 iron, but I don't recommend it for the Sunday golfer. Because it has virtually no loft at all, comparable to the putter, it's almost impossible for the average high-handicap player to get a clean, sweet shot with it. He's better off in every case to use the 4- or 5-woods.

But now that we have these beautifully wrought tools of the game, let's take a closer look at them. Before we even go out to the practice tee, it's a good idea to know what you've got in the bag, and why.

Starting with the woods, let's consider the driver. This is the longest club in the bag, running from 42 to 44 inches from the heel of the club to the top of the shaft. This is the big boomer and, as far as I'm concerned, the most important instrument in the kit. Why? Because I regard the drive as the game's Big Shot. You can talk all you like about putting and chipping, and this shot and that one. But if you can't put the ball out there in playing position, all the rest of the words can be sung to the tune of "Somewhere Over the Rainbow."

Table of Distances and Degrees of Loft

Club	Average distance		Degrees of loft
Woods	Men	Women	
No. 1	220 yds.	190 yds.	11 degrees
No. 2*	210 yds.	180 yds.	14 degrees
No. 3	200 yds.	170 yds.	17 degrees
No. 4	190 yds.	160 yds.	20 degrees
No. 5	180 yds.	150 yds.	23 degrees
Irons			
No. 1*	190 yds.	160 yds.	19 degrees
No. 2	180 yds.	150 yds.	23 degrees
No. 3	170 yds.	140 yds.	27 degrees
No. 4	160 yds.	130 yds.	31 degrees
No. 5	150 yds.	120 yds.	35 degrees
No. 6	140 yds.	110 yds.	39 degrees
No. 7	130 yds.	100 yds.	43 degrees
No. 8	120 yds.	90 yds.	47 degrees
No. 9	110 yds.	80 yds.	51 degrees
No. 10*	90 yds.	70 yds.	55 degrees
No. 11*	90 yds.	70 yds.	59 degrees
Wedge	100 yds.	70 yds.	55 degrees
Putter	—	—	1 degree

* Not commonly used

Your irons are bought and replaced in sets. Generally speaking, so are your other woods. But two clubs are purchased, discarded, replaced on an individual basis to suit your own special sense of fitness. These are the driver and the putter. Both clubs must be right for the player. If you don't feel comfortable with that driver (or that putter), you'll never hit a lick with either club until you replace it.

So, before you strike off down the fairway, be happy with your driver. Maybe you prefer a heavy head? A thin, whippy shaft? A long shaft? Small head? Find a driver you like the *feel* of. If you're buying a full set of woods, be sure the driver is right. You can learn to live with the other woods in the set. You can adapt to them. But the driver has to be the right driver for you, right at the outset.

The No. 2 wood has lost much of its usefulness in recent years. By that, I mean its usefulness has diminished with the growing usefulness of the more versatile No. 4 and No. 5 woods. The No. 2 is something of a relic of yesterday. It's the old "brassie," originally conceived—oddly enough—as a trouble club, which gradually evolved into the club used for fairway play when you're blessed with a clean lie and you hope to approximate the flight of the tee shot without the help of a wooden peg to get the ball off the ground. The length of the shaft is the same as the driver, but the face of the club is set back an additional 3 degrees to get the ball into flight more quickly.

I suggest discarding the No. 2 wood because the 3-wood will give you just about the same distance and the No. 3, with an even greater angle of loft in the face, is a safer club to use. With the No. 3 wood, the ball doesn't have to be perched up there, winking and smiling at you from a lush fairway. It will still come sailing out of a tight lie, eager to fly. The 3- and 4-woods are about 1 inch shorter in the shaft than the No. 1 and No. 2.

For a third wood, I would recommend carrying a No. 4 wood. I consider this club one of the most versatile clubs in your bag. It will play you out of situations which, in another day, would call for one of those long irons that are so treacherous in the hands of an unskilled player. The No. 4 wood will give you all the distance of a No. 1 iron and, frankly, I don't know a dozen professionals who can play a 1-iron with any degree of razor-sharp consistency.

The No. 4 wood, too, will get you home on some of those long par-3 holes that are just beyond your comfortable iron range. Behind the driver, the No. 4 unquestionably ranks second in importance among your woods.

A relative newcomer in the bag is the No. 5 wood, again about one inch shorter in the shaft than the 3 and the 4. It's a good club, very popular among the women professionals who need a "get there" club and lack the wrist and arm power to get full measure out of the longer irons. In the hands of a player who likes it, masters it and trusts it, it's a real killer. Try it on for size. If you get on with it okay, carry it and leave the No. 2 iron at home.

It might be advisable to take a moment right here and comment briefly on an important difference between men's and women's clubs. Men usually prefer X and S shafts, but women should get rather softer club shafts with more whip to them. The woman golfer should try for the widest possible arc to build up maximum club-head speed at impact. Ordinarily, they have very good timing and a natural sense of rhythm. Because they recognize their physical limitations they rarely try to overpower the ball, depending on a slow and graceful swing to accomplish their purpose.

For this reason, women usually find a great deal of satisfaction in mastering the fairway woods. These clubs enable them to deal on nearly even terms with golf courses that are designed and built to test the longer masculine hitters. Someday I would like to construct a course expressly for the woman golfer, measured to her game. Meanwhile, her long woods are her best friends out there on the regulation courses.

Now there are No. 6 and No. 7 woods on the market, but I don't see much point in discussing them because, the first thing you know, we'll be back to the years 1421 A.D., playing entirely with wooden "spoons" again. But, after all, it's just a game and the idea is to enjoy it and score to the best of your ability. If these grotesqueries of the club-maker's art make you happy and, above all, if they help you score —by all means carry them in good health!

Turning now to the irons, let's give the 1-iron to the baby as a teething toy. He'll get more use out of it. Unless you're prepared to enter a period of prayer and fasting and daily practice with it, you'll never bat better than .250 with that club. The club face is too small and the "sweet spot" too elusive for the weekend golfer. And, if you're going to carry three woods, wedge, sand iron and putter, you won't have room for it in your bag anyway. The fourteen-club rule will catch up with you.

The so-called "long" irons are the Nos. 1, 2 and 3. Some people include the No. 4, but since this is an arbitrary arrangement, let's assign the 4 to the medium-range irons. All your irons are stepped down in shaft length and set back at a steeper degree of loft as we move down the scale in hitting length. At the same time, the face—or hitting area—increases with the angle of loft.

So, the No. 1 iron has the longest shaft and the smallest face of all the irons. As I pointed out above, this is enough to discourage its popular use among the high-handicap players. The No. 2 iron is a little better, but not much. It's a great club in the hands of the professional simply because there are occasions when it's the *only* club for the shot at hand. Only a low-handicap amateur, product of hundreds of hours on the practice tee, will recognize and appreciate the difference between the 2- and the 3-irons.

Mastery of the No. 2 iron should be a challenge and a goal for the earnest student of the game, but of the three long irons, you will probably spend most of your time with the No. 3. This is the old mid-iron of once-upon-a-time, and king of the long irons. For all practical purposes, this ticket will get you in just about any place the No. 2 will—and probably will become an old friend much sooner.

The Nos. 4, 5 and 6 are your medium irons, the "get-home" clubs. With the longer irons, you're firing for distance and range. You're lining in on the green, but you're stretching —and hoping. When you pull one of the middle irons out of the bag, the name of the game is Accuracy. You're not playing for a slot on the fairway and hoping for a happy run or a lucky bounce. You're zeroed in on the green and you expect to drop it there. In the old days, the blessed mashie handled these shots.

Now we move along down to the short irons, Nos. 7, 8 and 9. We're in the old niblick range. Distance has ceased to be a factor in our calculations; it's all accuracy now, and timing and delicacy of touch become critical considerations. We're in the Land of the Three-Quarter Swing. It's not a question of hitting the green now—or shouldn't be. We're homing in on that *pin*—or lofting the ball over a hazard of one sort or another. These are pitching irons.

As often as not, when you're within pitching range, you'll prefer to go to the wedge. I can't imagine what the world was like before the development of the wedge. Uncle Tony is a pitching and wedge-playing fool. I've been passionately in love with the wedge for years, but she's a sweetheart I have to share with a lot of other guys. The pros probably spend more hours working with that wedge than any other club in the bag. Believe me, it's a real salvation iron when you're out there in the cold, cruel scramble for pesos and you're trying to snatch a par out of a shambles of a hole. The wedge is the club that bails you out, and slides you up to that pin for a blow-in.

The less said about the putter the better. Here is an instrument of torture, designed by Tantalus, and forged in the devil's own smithy. It can be a magic wand or a writhing snake, depending on whether or not the ball is popping into the hole on a given day. Galahad's quest for the Holy Grail was just a cursory glance compared with the feverish search that goes on constantly among golfers for that one putter with the golden touch.

No club in the bag has been so hammered, twisted, bent and shaped to so many grotesque forms. No other shot in the game has been played with so many contortions of the human body. As Ben Hogan says, putting really isn't golf at all. Golf, he claims, is a game played in the air. Putting is a ground game. Both Lloyd Mangrum and Francis Ouimet agree that, if they had to start all over again, they'd begin with the putter and work their way up to the wood clubs. I know some professionals who say, if they had to start all over again with the putter, they'd take up jai alai, or underwater demolition.

Incidentally, in dating the dawn of popular American golf from Ouimet's 1913 victory in the U.S. Open, we tend to forget that an American named Walter Travis went over to Britain nine years earlier, in 1904, and won the British Amateur championship. If you think Ouimet's upset defeat of Vardon and Ray caused a popular stir here, you can imagine the shock wave that rolled across the Firth of Forth when the upstart American tamed the British tigers on their own veldt.

After a bit of soul-searching, the elders of British golf decided that the real villain of the piece was Travis's "Schenectady" putter, a hammer-headed device designed along the lines of the croquet mallet—and swung the same way. There was a lot of hue and considerable cry about the whole nasty business, and the upshot was a quick rewrite of the Rules of Golf to outlaw the Schenectady putter. The revised rule decreed that the shaft of the putter had to join the clubhead somewhere east or west of the center-line of the head.

Of course, something had to be done, sooner or later, or you'd have had guys out there lining up putts with billiard cues! Not that this hasn't been done, either. For that matter, not too many years ago there was a hustling type of fellow who bobbed around on the fringe of the Hollywood movie colony and promoted a lot of martini money by performing legendary feats on the golf course. If memory serves me faithfully, he would offer to beat you playing with a rake and a broom. And he could do it!

Getting back to putters, at least one mad genius came up with a pendulum-type machine with a putter blade attachment. It was illegal, naturally, but it did manage to divorce the fickle nervous system completely from the putting process.

And there was the late Leo Diegel who used to come so unsprung over a putt that he developed a jackknife stance and arms-akimbo posture, both forearms running horizontally east and west, and used to repeat to himself, "I'm a pendulum . . . I'm a pendulum . . ." I think this was how the Method school of acting got started.

Getting the Swing of It

The evolution of the golf club and ball has been accompanied by a steady downward drift in tournament scoring. The first time the British Open championship was played at 72 holes, back in 1892, an amateur named Harold Hilton won it at Muirfield with a score of 305. Seventy years later, playing at Troon, Arnold Palmer won the same tournament with a record low score of 276.

The Open was first played at 72 holes at St. Andrews in 1895 and won by J. H. Taylor with 326. In 1964, over the same Old Course at St. Andrews, I had to score 279 to win. In the intervening years, the Open was played ten times at St. Andrews with these scores:

1900—J. H. Taylor, 309
1905—James Braid, 318
1910—James Braid, 299
1921—Jock Hutchison (USA), 296
1927—Robert T. Jones, Jr. (USA), 285
1933—Denny Shute (USA), 292

1939—Richard Burton, 290
1946—Sam Snead (USA), 290
1955—Peter Thomson (Australia), 281
1959—Bobby Locke (South Africa), 279

Bob Jones's winning 285 at St. Andrews in 1927 is especially noteworthy because it was Jones, three years later, who turned out the first set of perfectly matched and balanced irons for the A. G. Spalding Co. He and Spalding established the first table of weights and measures, and fixed the angle of loft, for golf clubs. And that was the end of the mashie and the niblick, generic terms applied to clubs that fell into rather broad classifications determined by the shape and degree of loft of the club face.

The development of the steel shaft and the matched set produced a revolution in golf comparable to the introduction of the modern ball. It led directly to a surge of popularity for the game in America and eventual domination by the American players. Almost overnight, the new clubs transformed the old masters into skilled performers with obsolete tools.

The old hickory shafts, with their combination of whip and twist (torsion), gave each club a distinct individuality. The old champion had to be a virtuoso with several instruments. Quite suddenly, he was replaced by an entirely new concept of the game—a basic swing which produced all the necessary strokes.

Now clubs were numbered 1, 2, 3 and so on down the line. In theory, at least, if each club were swung by a machine, it would play to a fixed length and the ball would traverse a specific trajectory. All that was needed now to reduce the game to a simple mechanical process was to develop a human machine which could repeat the same swing endlessly.

And so the fine art of striking a golf ball became a search for a method to lock the student's swing into the so-called "groove." Happily, human beings aren't robots, and it's the margin for human error which will always preserve the

" 'umblin' " nature of the game. Golf tournaments are almost never won by the winner. They're lost by the losers. A round of golf is just a brave flirtation with disaster. The success or failure of the round is measured by the number of shots that are missed.

Still and all, the mass production of perfectly balanced clubs produced a major revolution in golf—and particularly in the United States, where the market for these matched clubs was virtually insatiable. The 1930s marked a point of departure from the beautifully fluid swing of the old masters. The American tournament professional, honed to razor edge on a twelve-month tournament wheel and clawing for survival in a competitive jungle, began developing a blocky and explosive style of play. In the late 1930s and in the postwar years, the Americans simply demolished their British rivals in the biennial Ryder Cup matches, prompting one despairing British golf writer, after the 1949 matches at Ganton, England, to describe the Yanks as "golfing automatons."

Meanwhile, the American amateurs were shaping their game along the lines drawn by their professional colleagues and their domination of the Walker Cup matches has been even more overwhelming.

We've come a long way since 1900, when J. H. Taylor scored a 309 to win the Open at St. Andrews—and when the well-dressed gentleman shrugged himself into a heavy scarlet jacket before sallying forth to the links for a go at the ancient game. To me, it's not surprising that Ouimet knocked off Vardon and Ray. Studying pictures of the three, I'm astonished that the two Englishmen could get around the course four times in 304 strokes bundled up in those damn tweed jackets!

America introduced shirt-sleeve golf. Inevitably, this led to a modification of the rather upright swing of the jacket-bound British classicists. The American golfer's swing became a more compact thing, more flat-footed. It has evolved gradually into what is now known as the "Square Method." The Square Method of hitting a golf ball is entirely logical and can be stated quite simply. It's based on the theory that, if the club face meets the ball squarely and follows through on that plane, the ball can't go anywhere but straight.

The old technique of "pronating," or rolling, the wrists is dead. The wrists must be regarded as a hinge. When the ball is struck, the back of the left hand should be squarely facing the target, and it must continue to go out toward the target until the wrist swings on its hinge as the hands carry the club up to a high finish.

The stance is square. In almost every instance, we'll play the ball straightaway, just off the left heel. On the backswing, we'll carry that clubhead directly back from the ball as far as we can because we expect to return along that same line.

We're going to try to keep things very simple because hitting a golf ball is not a particularly complicated piece of business. As the late Macdonald Smith, a California pro, used to describe the swing, "All you do is wind up—then unwind." That's a real over-simplification, of course. So was Babe Zaharias's advice to the ladies: "Just loosen up your girdle and swing!" But the point each was making is this: The act of hitting a stationary object with a club has been performed by human beings since the time of the Piltdown Man. There's nothing difficult about it. It only gets complicated when you stop and ask yourself, "What am I doing?"

In the following pages we're going to place a golf club in your hands, show you how to use it and then lead you out onto the golf course and show you how to play it.

During the last several decades we've seen about five strokes a round whittled off the winning scores in the British and U.S. Open championships. In these pages we expect to shave at least as many strokes off your handicap.

So let's tee up . . .

POSITION OF THE BALL I believe in keeping the game as simple as possib
With a few exceptions, I prefer to play all shots directly off the left heel, or close
that position. And why not? There's no point in complicating matters by maki
adjustments in the arc of the swing for the various clubs.

THE STANCE When you stand up to the ball, it's important that you feel comfortable. Weight is comfortably balanced on the balls of the feet and the knees are slightly flexed, just enough to unlock them for easy lateral movement. Don't squat and don't stoop over the shot.

2

How to hit a golf ball

The Grip

Golf is a game that is measured in yards, but the difference between a hit and a miss is calipered in micro-millimeters. Catch the ball squarely on the "sweet spot" of the club and you're rewarded with a fine shot. Miss it by a hair, and it's over the river and through the woods to grandmother's house we go.

In short, it's a game of delicate timing and acute sensitivity that begins when you pick up the club. They tell me it was pure pleasure just to watch Walter Hagen draw a club from the bag and balance it lightly in his fingers before standing up to a shot. His touch was feather-light and he handled the club with affection and artistry, the way a concert master handles his baton, or a surgeon his scalpel.

A baseball bat is held with the hands. So are oars. But you hold a golf club with your fingers. *In* your hands, but *with* your fingers. This is important. If you hold the club like a cleaver, you'll play like a butcher. Hold it like a suction pump and you'll "plumber" the shot.

The clubhead has to meet the ball squarely at the bottom of the swing arc, when it's traveling at maximum speed. The only way you can know this is happening is through the fingers, which transmit this information to the hands and, by neuro-telegraph, to the brain. Without this knowledge there is no control, and without control you might as well be swinging a buggy whip.

This is what's known as having "live" hands—meaning they are alert to what is happening at the far end of the shaft, the business end. Without this sensitive finger control of the club, timing and rhythm are just two unrelated words in the dictionary. The golf swing is an exercise in timing and rhythm, and, in the words of the popular song of another generation, "It don't mean a thing if you ain't got that swing . . ."

Let's get our hands on a club.

Take your driver and place the clubhead on the turf behind an imaginary ball. This is very close to the actual position of the clubhead when it passes through the striking zone. Now you must grip the club so your hands will guide it naturally into this position on impact.

Support the club lightly with your right hand so the butt end of the shaft is about 8 to 10 inches from you and pointing toward the pit of your stomach. This should place the club very close to the correct angle of attack. Now place the palm of your left hand against the club grip so the back of the hand is squarely facing the imaginary target. Remember what we said about the Square Method? We want the back of that left hand square against the line of flight when the clubhead meets the ball.

Now let's fold the left hand over the grip so the butt of the club is cushioned against the pad of muscle on the heel of the hand and the shaft runs diagonally down across the palm and the upper joint of the left index finger. We wrap the hand around the club, gripping the shaft firmly with the last two fingers (ring and little fingers) of the hand. The

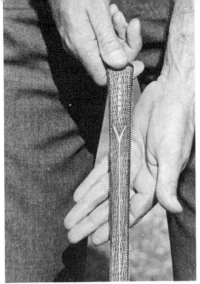
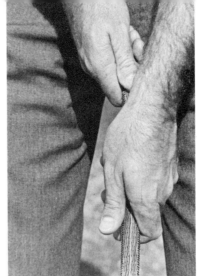

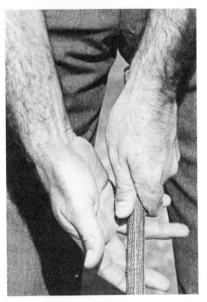

THE GRIP You *hold* the club in the left hand, but *grip* it only with the ring and little fingers. These "pressure points," squeezing the shaft against the heel pad of the hand, *anchor* the swing. *Control* and *sensitivity* are centered largely in the *index* and *middle* fingers of the right hand, which, with the *thumb,* constitute the other pressure points of the grip.

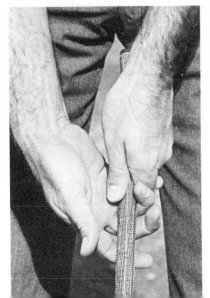
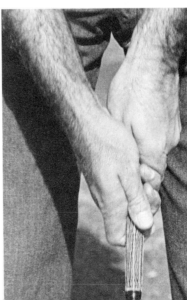

other fingers are only supporting the shaft lightly, and the thumb is resting on the shaft so the V formed by the thumb and left index finger is pointing toward the right shoulder.

At this point, you are *holding* the club in the left hand, but *gripping* it only with the last two fingers. These are called the "pressure points" and this means just what it sounds like. These two fingers, squeezing the shaft against the heel pad of the hand, actually *anchor* the swing. *Control* and *sensitivity* are centered in the *index* and *middle fingers* of the right hand which, with the *thumb* of the right hand, constitute the other pressure points of the grip.

These five fingers, working together, actually swing the club. The hands only respond to their demands for support and force. We'll discuss this further, but let's get the right hand on the club first . . .

Place the right hand around the shaft so the left thumb fits snugly into the hollow formed by the palm and thumb pad of the right hand. The V formed by the right thumb and index finger will point toward the right shoulder. We grip the shaft with the thumb and first two fingers of the right hand. The ring finger of the right hand is a supporting finger, like the left index and middle fingers.

What about the little finger of the right hand?

The so-called "Vardon," or overlapping, grip is used almost universally today—and with good reason. It links the two hands, physically, so they function together, as one. And we might as well stop right here and get one matter settled before we go any further. *The golf swing is not a one-hand swing.* I don't care what anyone says about hitting the ball with this hand or the other hand, or controlling with the left or right. It takes two to tango and two to swing. Those two hands have to be working together or, man, you're playing another game entirely!

The overlapping grip simply means you lay that little finger of the right hand in the groove between the left index and middle fingers. It's a very comfortable fit after you're used to it. Ironically, this is the grip ascribed to Harry Vardon and he never used it, really. The true Vardon grip

IT TAKES TWO TO SWING This is the Vardon, or overlapping, grip, which is use almost universally today. Actual linkage of the right little finger with the left inde finger permits the two hands to function as one. Remember: it takes two to tang and two to swing!

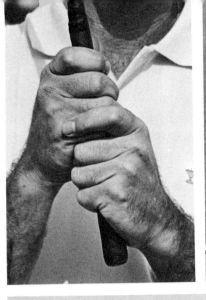

was a true overlapping one, with the little finger of the right hand crooked right over the knuckle of the left index finger. For Vardon, with his enormous hands, this was the overlapping grip. For the rest of us coming after him, the overlapping grip became sort of an "interleaving" grip, with the right little finger slipping down into the valley between the other two fingers.

This is the grip which is employed by 99 of 100 golfers today. There are still a few, like Nicklaus and Sarazen, who prefer the interlocking grip in which the right little finger and left index finger actually link, or interlock. Theoretically, it is more comfortable for persons with smaller hands who cannot use the overlapping grip. I find this argument a little hard to fathom, but you're welcome to try on the interlocking grip for size. The important thing is to (1) feel comfortable, (2) grip the club only at the finger pressure points and (3) link those hands so they will work as one.

A third method of holding the club is the so-called "baseball" grip which, in effect, is a modification of the hand grip used to hold a baseball bat. This one, too, is basically a finger grip, but there is no actual linkage of the two hands. Art Wall and Bob Rosburg use it, but I don't recommend it for adoption. It's just doing it the hard way, making you set up a whole new sensory pattern to bring the two hands into play together.

If you have a sound grip, with the hands working together and responding alertly to the pressure needs of the fingers, you should now swing the club through the striking arc and feel the drag of the clubhead at the far end of the shaft—as if the shaft were flexible and you were swinging a weight at the end of it. And, actually, this is the case. When your grip tells you this, you're ready to hit a golf ball.

Standing Up to the Ball

When anyone asks how far he should stand from the ball, I'm always reminded of the old wheeze about, How long is a piece of string? The answer to that one, of course, is, Long enough to reach both ends. And the answer to the other silly question is just as obvious: Stand close enough to reach the ball with room enough to swing.

Without making a federal case of it, let's stand up to the ball.

When you address the ball, your weight should be comfortably on the balls of your feet and your knees slightly flexed. Don't squat, and don't stoop over the shot. The trunk is reasonably upright and the knees are just flexed enough to unlock them for free movement during the swing.

From this position, the face of the club should lie squarely behind the ball without reaching for it, or feeling cramped. You should be nicely balanced so you can swing freely without lunging forward or falling away.

We're going to play nearly all our shots straightaway. That is, we're going to tee the ball on a line with the left heel. For some shots, as we near the green, we'll position the ball a little farther back of that line—but never more than 2 or 3 inches.

We'll take our stance by placing the club face behind the ball, squarely in line with the target; then we'll take up a position facing the ball with our feet toeing an imaginary line that parallels the line of flight. I like to play most shots from the same foot position, with the toes pointing outward at an angle of about 20 degrees. If we picture our position in the center of a giant clock dial, the toes would be pointing to "five minutes to one o'clock."

There's a very good reason for pointing the shoes at "five minutes to one" and not "ten minutes to two" or "twelve o'clock high." You see, the heart of the golf swing is the knee action. If your feet are planted and pointing dead ahead, the right foot is going to restrict your pivot on the backswing, and the left foot will choke off your follow-through. Open the feet wider than about 20 degrees and you run into the same problem in reverse—the anchored left foot restrains you on the backswing, and if you try to swing through with the right foot pointing off toward New Hampshire, you'll wind up with a double hernia.

FOOT POSITION Correct foot position is essential for a fluid swing. Toes should point to "five minutes to one o'clock" on an imaginary clock dial. This position permits a smooth hip pivot. A wider angle between the feet would result in a restricted backswing, anchored by the left foot. Point them straight ahead and the right foot will restrict the swing.

The foot position is determined by the need to pivot the upper part of the body a full 180 degrees.

You can "open" or "close" your stance by drawing the left foot back an inch or two from the line of attack, or by drawing back the right foot. Opening or closing the stance doesn't alter the basic foot position—that is, the position of the feet in relation to each other. It is simply an adjustment of the position to deal with a special circumstance. The chronic slicer, for instance, often finds prompt relief by closing his stance. By drawing back his right foot he unblocks his right side completely and makes it easier for him to find the "inside-out" swing groove he's looking for.

On the other hand, the persistent hooker may compensate by opening his stance and clearing his left side. Strangely, this opening of the left side tends to restrain the hooker's inclination to turn on the shot. The open stance also may be used when you want to hit a deliberate slice (around an obstacle). And we usually open the stance somewhat as we move down to the pitching and chipping irons because now there is no need for a full backswing. These shots are played with a shorter arc and, by setting up an unnatural block of the right side, we tend to enforce a more compact swing.

The feet should be spaced at about shoulder width for the full hit. Again, for the shorter irons, the feet may be brought closer together as we open the stance and "crowd" the shot. A wider stance than shoulder width is self-defeating because, like the wider angle of the feet, it locks the knees and restricts the swing.

A good way to take your stance is to perform a deep knee bend. The foot position which gives you the most secure balance is your correct stance for hitting a golf ball. If the feet are too wide apart you'll tend to topple backward; if they're set too close together, you'll sense a lack of balance.

The key to a sound stance is balance. When you're standing up to the ball correctly you should have a strong sense of stability, as if your center of gravity is located in your bottom and your weight is evenly distributed on both legs and solidly supported in the heels. I like to think of the billiken as a model. The billiken, you know, is a round-bottomed figure you can push over from any side and which will rock back erect again. That's because it's weighted in the base and has a dead-level center of gravity.

Like Leo Diegel used to tell himself he was a pendulum, try telling yourself you're a billiken. Who knows? Maybe you are!

Your knees are flexed, but not relaxed. There should be some tension in your legs, a springiness. In fact, try to think of your knees not so much as being flexed, but rather unlocked from their sockets—ready to move laterally in support of the body pivot.

Your body should bend at the waist—but only slightly, enough to place you within comfortable reach of the ball. A short person will tend to bend a little less than a tall one. But, whatever you do, don't hunch over the shot. If you do, you're standing too close to the ball. Stooped shoulders are out this season. Actually, the line from the base of the spine to the head should be perfectly straight. The inclination at the waist should be just enough to make the out-thrust rear end the most prominent feature of your profile as you stand up to the shot.

In this position, you should have a secure sense of balance. You should feel your weight distributed through the muscles along the back of the legs and calves. With the club soled behind the ball, you should be able to rock back on your heels and press your toes against the tops of your shoes without altering the position of the hands and the club. Bear in mind, when you swing the club, that it's going to pass through the impact zone at a speed approaching 100 miles an hour. Unless you're firmly rooted in your stance, the force of the swing is going to pull or push you off balance.

As you address the ball, the left arm should be extended —not rigid, but reasonably straight and firm. This left arm is the radius of the swing arc. It guides the club into the backswing and back into the ball. You can't very well execute an accurate arc with a floppy radius. You never saw a bicycle with rubber spokes, did you?

PROFILE OF A GOLFER The body should bend slightly from the waist as you address the ball. But don't stoop! Line from the base of the spine to the head should be quite straight. Weight is evenly distributed on both feet and the knees are unlocked. Bear in the mind that the clubhead will flash through the striking zone at a speed of about 100 miles an hour. You have to have a secure sense of balance to maintain control of it at that speed.

Your shoulders should be square to the line of flight, but the right shoulder is going to be slightly lower than the left. This is because the right hand is placed a little lower on the shaft. But again, a word of warning against exaggerating the shoulder dip. Let's not develop curvature of the spine trying to get that right shoulder down. I wouldn't bother to mention it at all except that it does happen, and I don't want you worrying about it.

It's more important to worry about your head, as I keep telling missionaries who are leaving for the Congo. A lot has been written and said about not moving the head. This is misleading. The head *does* move during the swing. It *has* to, as we'll see when we get into a discussion of the swing itself. But the head doesn't move during the *backswing*. From the moment you stand up to that ball until the clubhead approaches its peak speed on the downswing, your head is the one part of your body that is not in motion. It's the stabilizer, the built-in gyroscope around which all the various forces are grouping for the big explosion.

The Swing

I suspect that, if anyone wanted to hole up in the public library and run a word count by subject matter on the literature of the twentieth century, he would find that the most popular subjects are sex, crime and the golf swing—and not necessarily in that order.

Before we go any further, let's have a clear understanding. You're not going to find a golf swing in a book. You're not going to put this little volume aside and walk out on the golf course bathed in radiance, tee up a ball and be mistaken for Anthony Lema—or anyone else who hits golf balls for a living. For that matter, you don't read a thesis on wind instruments and then go downtown and audition with the Philharmonic, or spend the morning browsing in the library, then ramble out to the stadium armed with book knowledge and volunteer to play middle linebacker for the Green Bay Packers.

Timing and rhythm mean everything in the golf swing. These are natural qualities that can be sharpened and refined. But, if there is nothing there to begin with, we're in trouble right off the bat. Some people are born with a little metronome buried in a crevasse of the brain. Others spend their lives knocking over lamps every time they reach for a cigarette. I have an idea the first time young Ted Williams faced a pitcher on a San Diego sandlot, he nearly tore the other kid's head off with a line drive. Then I've known others who would have to have instruction before they could hit the living room rug with a handful of birdshot.

If you are blessed with muscular coordination, a natural sense of rhythm, you can hit a golf ball right now. Maybe not as far as you might, or always in the right direction. But the act of hitting the ball holds no mystery for you. When I say, "Let's keep this thing simple," I can see you sitting there, nodding your head in full agreement.

On the other hand, if you were born without that little subconscious tick-tock called "timing," no assurance from me is going to keep the golf swing from becoming the most complicated essay in physics since Archimedes sat down to work out the principle of flotation. These people have to learn to hit a golf ball with a manufactured swing. For them, I will try to dissect the swing so they can manufacture it in segments and then put together a reasonable facsimile.

For the fortunate ones, blessed with the gift of muscular music, this breakdown of the swing into its component parts will offer a useful checklist that will help them to refine their game and smooth out any wrinkles in their swing.

I'm told by those who spend a lot of time studying such things that I have a highly stylized swing. I don't know. Like most golfers who play at the top tournament level, to me, swinging a golf club is something that comes as naturally as breathing.

Certain features of my swing have been pointed out to me and sequence photographs I've seen tend to confirm them. One knowledgeable British writer remarked on what he called the "absolute smoothness" of my swing, and on the fact that the pace of the swing never varies from shot to shot, and from club to club.

Dai Rees, the veteran Welsh Ryder Cup player, says he was impressed, watching me at St. Andrews, by the simplicity of my game. He observed that I just walked up to the ball and hit it as if it were the most natural thing in the world.

I think both observations are valid and are directly related. They explain why I harp on the theme of keeping the game simple and uncomplicated. Because, as I pointed out earlier, I nearly always play the ball in the same relative position, it follows logically that there is no earthly reason to vary the tempo or the arc of my swing. This is keeping it simple.

There are other unique features of my own swing which we'll develop in a mechanical breakdown of the golf swing. For instance, my left arm remains inordinately firm and extended throughout the backswing. My wrists don't cock fully until the hands start dragging the club back into the downswing. There's more than the normal amount of knee action in my body pivot, and my head and shoulders recoil like a battery of deck cannons when I hit the ball.

Are these personal characteristics good or bad? Should you adopt them? I wouldn't recommend that you model your game on anyone's. But the fact that I've had some degree of success with a style and method that is my own suggests that it's worth examining very closely. Behind the style has to be a fundamental logic in the swing. The exaggerated firmness of my left arm, for example, is ideally suited to my physical structure—and blends into the pattern of my swing. For you, such an exaggeration may not be suitable at all. But the *theory* of the straight left arm is sound. It is one of the building blocks of the golf swing.

Let's see what happens during the golf swing . . .

There are two things we expect from an efficient golf swing, two things we keep in mind throughout. First, we want to develop the greatest possible clubhead speed at the instant of impact. Second, we hope to bring the clubhead into the ball squarely along the line of flight. In other words, we want to hit the ball precisely and squarely so it will leave the club-face with no place to go but away and out.

To accomplish this we have to build a mental picture of the path we want the clubhead to follow, from address to the top of the backswing and down again—sort of a "road map" of the swing. And to put the clubhead on this path we have to start by taking it back low and along a perfectly straight line for at least a full foot. Why? Because you want to bring the clubhead back along this same track when you hit the ball.

Remember those two points above all: Picture the path of the swing in your mind, and start the club back along that path. These are the keystones in the structure of the swing.

Now, let's go back and start at the beginning of the swing and tick off the principal check points.

When we stand up to that ball, the first thing we're going to do is to get a good, comfortable, well-balanced stance. Then we're going to get our fingers and hands moving, to alert them to the job. Remember, we're holding that club in our hands but *with* our fingers. Now, as we stand up to the ball, we'll waggle the clubhead a few times, just to remind the fingers of the "feel" of the clubhead, to sense the weight at the far end of the shaft.

The next step is the Forward Press. This is a subtle, barely perceptible surge of the body against a braced left leg, usually carrying the hands to a point slightly ahead of the ball. Not every player uses the Forward Press. Not everyone finds a use for it. But, for most, it serves a double purpose. First, for many, it starts the hidden timing clock ticking in the subconscious. Second, it serves very nicely to get the hands in motion smoothly and fluidly so the clubhead can start back from the ball gracefully and effortlessly.

Now, we're going to take that clubhead back along a flat plane—straightaway—for a distance of 12 to 18 inches. The worst thing you can do at this point is to "pick up" the club, the way you'd lift a baseball bat to your shoulder. We want that clubhead, or blade, moving back, slowly and smoothly, along a track that is absolutely square against the line of flight.

To guard against lifting the club, and to put the clubhead along its widest possible arc, we make a conscious effort to extend the left arm. In fact, we don't really draw the club back at all—we sort of *push it back* along this low plane with the straight left arm. At this point, the right arm, with the biceps brushing against your side, is only playing a supporting role, going along for the ride.

The left arm, firmly extended and thrusting the clubhead back along this wide arc, is memorizing its function as the radius of the swing arc. In a moment, it's going to guide the clubhead back along the same path to make contact squarely with the ball.

At this point we encounter one of the curious apparent contradictions that can make the swing such an occult science if you don't take it in stride. It's this: While you're actively *pushing* the club back with the left arm and hand, the fingers should be reporting a strong sensation of "dragging" the clubhead back. There's no contradiction, really, because the thrusting sensation is related to the action of the arm, originating in the shoulder. The drag, experienced by the pressure-sensitive fingers, is related to psychic phenomena which we'll call, quite simply, "getting ready to hit."

Just as a pitcher winds up to throw the ball and a batter coils before swinging, so must we form a reservoir of power to be released on the swing. Think of the slingshot principle. The rubber bands are drawn back to their limit before being released. We should have the same sensation of drawing the clubhead back against some unseen force (inertia) that is holding it. As we steadily overcome this force and draw the clubhead back, we acquire a sense of strength and power, first in the fingers, then in the hands and wrists, and on through the entire body. This sense of strength and gathering force is translated readily into confidence, a critically important element in the swing.

THINGS BEGIN TO HAPPEN From the start of the backswing, the clubhead must be carried back along a flat plane for a distance of 12 to 18 inches. The worst thing you can do at this point is to "pick up" the club with the right hand. The club head (or blade) *must* move back slowly and smoothly along a track that is *absolutely square* against the path of flight.

As the clubhead continues back along this widest possible arc, the left arm continues firm and extended as far as it will go. In my case, as we've seen, the left arm remains virtually rigid all the way to the peak of the backswing, when the club approaches a horizontal position. The right arm remains tucked in to the body from shoulder to elbow, the forearm swinging open like a gate.

As the hands carry the club back, the body turns, like the hub of a wheel. The left knee bends in toward the ball while the right leg braces to support the shifting weight. The left shoulder, moving behind the thrust of the arm, rolls under the chin and is aligned with the right shoulder *squarely against the target.*

There is no rolling of the wrists on the backswing. The left wrist, in fact, is virtually locked in place until it is cocked on the downswing. The right wrist acts like a hinge, but never like a ball-socket. Thus, the club-face, which was placed squarely against the ball at the address, never has a chance to wander from the beaten track. Barring any complications, the face of the club is going to come down along the swing path in the same position it had going up. In the old days, it was considered the height of elegance to roll the wrists, coming and going. Why, I don't know. All it did was throw the face of the club wide open at the top of the backswing, and rolled it back into position coming down— sometimes. Like close-order drill, it was much ado about nothing.

Our next checkpoint is the drag of the clubhead on the downswing. As we are poised momentarily at the top of the backswing, our weight has to be transferred to the left side, which has to brace to receive it. This is a fluid movement, led by the left knee and followed instantly by the hips and shoulders. The sliding forward of the hips is accompanied by a swivel action, which begins slowly on the downswing, then gathers momentum as we come into the shot.

Again, the fingers are acutely sensitive to the drag of the clubhead as we start into the downswing. This dragging

EVER SEE A WHEEL WITH RUBBER SPOKES? Control of the swing rests with the left arm. This is the radius of the swing arc, the spoke of the wheel. Notice how I keep it almost rigid right to the top of the backswing. To maintain this firm and extended left arm, you must entertain a strong sense of *thrusting* the club back with the left arm, rather than *taking* it back with the hands.

THE HUB OF THE WHEEL As the hands carry the club back into striking position, the body turns like the hub of a wheel. The left knee bends in toward the ball while the right leg braces to support a shift in weight.

WRISTS ARE HINGES The classic swing of the nineteenth century, with its rolling (or "pronating") wrists, is as dead as Kelsey. The wrists perform like hinges, never like ball sockets. The left wrist, in fact, is virtually locked in position until it cocks on the start of the downswing. This cocking of the wrists takes place as the hands and fingers start pulling the club down into the swing. Imagine you're dragging on a bell cord.

sensation is real. We actually pull the club into the down-swing and (in my own case, at least) this pressure on the fingers is transmitted to the hands and the little metronome in the brain yells, "Now! Now it's time to cock the wrists!"

The left arm is still locked (if I may use a word that flies in the face of all golf authority) in that radial position and is drawing the club down along the same arc it followed in the backswing. Meanwhile, as the clubhead flashes down toward the ball, the right arm is straightening and the fingers, which have been running the show up to this time, turn to the hands and wrists and say, "Take over, boys—it's time to turn on the booster."

We have now reached the moment of truth. This is the payoff. We are about to hit the ball, and that's what it's all about. The clubhead is approaching its maximum speed— somewhere in the vicinity of 100 miles an hour. Now we're going to crack the whip and kick that speed up another notch.

What happens at this instant is critically important, and rarely understood. If you've read as much golf instruction as I have, you're probably saturated with warnings about moving the head. The head must never move, they scream. All I can say is that if your head doesn't move at impact you can't be holding a club in your hand. Not only does the head recoil, but so do the shoulders and the whole trunk of the body. They have to.

The principle of cracking the whip is fairly obvious. You've watched a line of skaters on a pond—or perhaps been a part of the human chain. The idea is for the leading skater to stop abruptly when the line has gathered sufficient forward speed, to wheel and brace himself. The No. 2 skater will make the turn almost as abruptly as the pivot man. Nos. 3 and 4 will describe slightly wider arcs and will gather some speed as their own forward momentum is augmented by the sudden drag of the wheeling pivot and No. 2. And so on, down the long line, until the skater at the far end finds his own forward speed sharply accelerated by the sweeping pull of the arc.

SOUND THE CHARGE! The forward surge of power starts with a firm planting of the left heel. This is followed instantly by a forward sliding movement of the hips as your weight is shifted to the left side, which then braces against the "flow of force" that begins pouring in behind the sweep of the club.

The point is, there can be no whip-cracking effect unless the original drawing force comes to an abrupt stop. As we bring the clubhead into the ball, the left arm changes its role from active to passive while the right hand and fingers are snapping the whip—kicking up the force and speed of the clubhead and getting the ultimate ounce of punch out of the stroke.

Now it's one of the basic Newtonian principles of physics that for every force there is a corresponding and reciprocating force. What that means, boiled down to 19th-hole English, is this: Unless you can set up a solid wall of resistance, the only way you can hope to stop a force in motion is to set up a corresponding and reciprocating force moving in the opposite direction.

The left side already is braced from the hip down. This is the solid wall of resistance we're hitting against. But there is no way we can anchor the trunk. So what happens? As we snap the clubhead into the ball, our shoulders have to recoil, carrying the head with them. This has the effect of bringing the right shoulder down and under, and bending the body *into* and *behind* the shot.

So there you have the picture at impact. The left wrist is square and solid, bracing against the right hand as the club whips through the bottom of its arc. The left side is firmly braced from hip to toe (although the left foot will roll over on the follow-through). The hips are swivelling and shoulders are turning forward to face the target. Both arms are perfectly straight now. The left is still guiding and controlling the sweep of the club and the right is carrying the flow of force from the larger back muscles to the hands.

The rest is anticlimax. You don't look up to follow the flight of the ball. If it lands on the green, someone will tell you. And someone will be happy to let you know if it goes in the pond. Let the head come up naturally as the body is drawn around by the force of the swing.

One important thing at this point, however: Keep that left arm firm. Don't let the elbow crumple. More shots have

THE NEWTONIAN LAW For every moving force there must be a corresponding and reciprocal force. We see this law at work in the golf swing. When we speak of keeping the head still during the swing, we're either talking nonsense or talking relatively. As this sequence of the swing clearly shows, head and upper body recoil noticeably as we build up a surge of power which explodes against the braced left side. The recoiling torso follows in behind the "flow of force" as we carry through to a smooth, high finish.

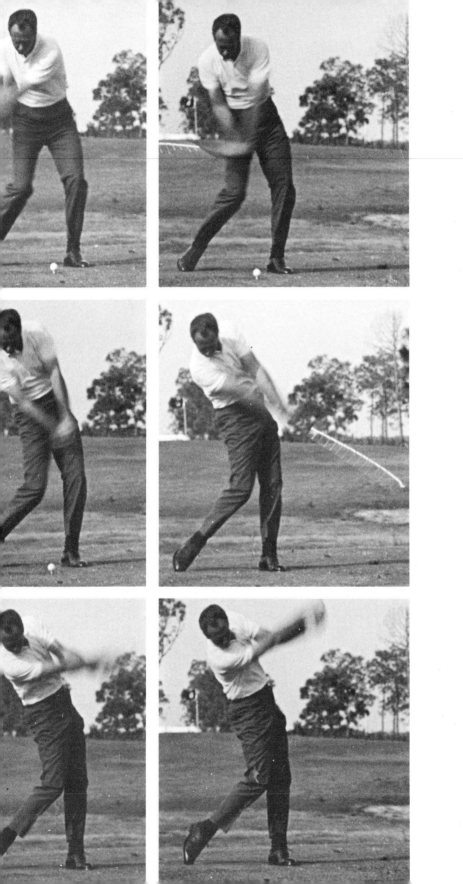

THE MOMENT OF TRUTH The "moment of truth" in golf is that instant when the clubhead, or blade, makes contact with the ball. Make sure you stay square with the shot all the way. At impact—and for a distance of at least 12 inches beyond that point—keep the back of the left hand squarely facing your target.

been ruined by a collapsing left elbow than by "peeking." In fact, a lot of fluffed shots are erroneously blamed on looking up when the real culprit was the floppy left elbow.

Remember to keep the back of the left hand square to the target all the way through the shot, and finish high— "throwing" the hands at the target, as they say.

That's the golf swing, broken down into its component parts. Each segment of the swing arc, in turn, can be dismantled and examined under the electronic microscope until a combat team from the sanitarium comes for you in the locker room and trusses you up like a roped dogie.

In galloping review, here's our checklist of critical factors in the swing:

1. The Waggle. Waggling the clubhead a few times as you take your stance alerts the fingers and establishes a sensory pattern.

2. The Forward Press. It serves two purposes: Sets your subconscious timer, and gets the hands moving so you can start the clubhead back smoothly and effortlessly.

3. The Drag. As the club is drawn back, the fingers should experience a strong sense of pulling against some force that is holding the clubhead. This serves to bring distant muscles into play, and should create an impression of a coil spring under gathering strain.

4. Left Arm Thrust. A firmly extended left arm literally *pushes* the club back along a low, straight plane as far as your position at the ball will permit. The idea is to establish the broadest possible arc for maximum clubhead speed, and to establish a firm radius for the swing.

5. Wrists Are Hinges. No rolling of the wrists as the club moves toward the top of the backswing. Left wrist remains firm throughout; right wrist acts like a door hinge and the club-face remains squarely facing the swing path.

6. Wrist Cock. When the club reaches a state of suspense at the top of the backswing, the fingers again start dragging it down. This feather-light pressure on the fingers is the signal to bring hand support to them for a firmer grip, and to cock the wrists for the coming whiplash.

7. The Brace. The "flow of force" begins with a planting of the left heel and a forward surge of the knees and hips, transferring the weight to the left side, which braces against the downswing. This is a positive action and should be heavily accented.

8. Cracking the Whip. Just before impact, the left hand and wrist—supported by the braced left side—brake to a stop. This sets up a wall of resistance for the right hand to whiplash the clubhead through the ball. The effect is to cause the head and trunk to recoil and follow in behind the shot.

9. Stay Square. At impact, and for a distance of at least 12 inches beyond, keep the back of the left hand squarely facing the hole.

10. Strong Left Elbow. Don't let the left elbow collapse as you carry through to a high finish, "throwing your hands at the target." Keep that left arm firm and extended until it *has to bend* naturally with the arc of the swing.

These are the Ten Commandments of the swing—five up, and five down. Obey them faithfully and you're a cinch to reach golfer's heaven. Some you can violate only under penalty of having your whole game shot to hell.

The swing we have described here, of course, is the full swing. As we move down the line with the shorter irons, naturally, we have to take a tuck in that swing. We have to modify it to deal with the special circumstances. We'll discuss these adjustments as we take up the various clubs. Right now, however, it's important that we clearly understand that when we talk about the Golf Swing, we're talking about the Big Sweep.

One final thought on the golf swing. Nobody ever hit a ball on the backswing. That is, not willingly. So there's no reason to get that clubhead up there in a hurry. Take lots of time. Carry that club back slowly and smoothly. The whole point of the backswing is to get the club into position to use it. Actually, nothing happens until you start dragging that club down again and cock the trigger.

So keep that backswing slow and silky.

THE TENTH COMMANDMENT No. 10 in my "Ten Commandments of the Swing" is this: Thou shalt not collapse thy left elbow. More shots are ruined by a collapsing left elbow than by "peeking." In fact, most bad shots attributed to looking up are actually elbow faults. Keep that left arm firm and extended until it has to yield naturally to the sweeping arc of the swing. Then let it go with the flow of force, and always "finish high."

Playing the Woods

Let's start with the driver. As I said earlier, I consider this the big club in the bag. It gets you out there, in position to play the game. If you can't get off the tee and down the fairway, you're not going to score. And if you can't swing the big stick, you might as well leave the rest of the tools in the closet because you can't swing them either.

When you swing the driver, you're executing the golf swing in its purest form. This is the way we've just finished describing it. There are no complicating factors. We don't take a divot. With this club we're always hitting off a wooden peg, so you never have a bad lie—and there's no excuse for missing the shot.

The No. 1 wood, or driver, is the heavy artillery, the long-range bomber. With the driver, happiness is a big hit with lots of roll. Accuracy is called by another name: control. All we're doing is playing for position—and trying to reach a point from where our next shot, in most cases, can get us home.

For the drive, we tee up the ball so the dead center of the ball meets the dead center of the club-face when we place the club behind the ball. We grip the club at the extreme end of the shaft because we want the longest possible arc in order to generate maximum clubhead speed for maximum distance.

We play the ball, as I pointed out, off the left heel because we want to get in behind it for a sweeping blow. We want to get that ball up and away, and the longer we can keep it in flight the more distance we'll get. To accomplish this we want to come into the ball squarely, along a low plane from a position straight back of the ball. This "square" hit that I emphasize will get the ball away on a rising trajectory with plenty of overspin, which converts into a good forward bounce and roll.

Don't ever baby this shot, or try to steer it. The drive is a big hit. Make it a big hit. Without breaking the tempo of your swing, put everything into it. Strive for maximum

THE FAIRWAY WOOD The No. 3 wood is your best bet for fairway carry. The shaft is a little shorter than the driver and the face of the club has an additional si degrees of loft for getting the ball up nicely out of the snug lies. You can choke dow on the grip with this club for better control without sacrificing any distance.

THE SHORT WOODS The short woods, Nos. 4 and 5, are useful tools for the amateur golfer whose game suffers from long-iron anemia—and for the senior player who finds the course beginning to stretch out for him. The shorter shafts call for a more upright swing, and we take a feather of turf with these shots. Instead of sweeping the ball off the grass, we move it back a little now and come into the ball just before we reach the bottom of the swing arc. It's almost as if we want to hammer the ball into the ground obliquely.

efficiency with every golf shot. With the drive this means you want to get all the mileage out of the club that you can, within your physical limitations. A lot of high-handicap players who are plagued with a chronic slice or a devilish hook fall into the trap of easing off on the shot. This is all right if it's just a temporary retreat from reality while the player rebuilds his swing, looking for the malfunction. But if he permits it to become a way of life, a compensatory adjustment in his swing, he's defeating the purpose of the club and not playing golf at all. We hit this one with everything we've got—and still maintain our balance.

We'll pass over the 2-wood and move along to the No. 3, or spoon. As we noted earlier, the shaft of the spoon is a little shorter than the driver, and the face of the club has another 6 degrees of loft. We're now dealing with fairway woods and we expect to encounter a variety of lies. The 3-wood is the logical choice when the ball is well set up on the fairway. Again, the position at the ball is the same as with the driver and the swing is still essentially a sweeping attack on the ball, meeting it flush and depending on the deeper loft of the club to get the ball up and winging.

If you encounter a snug lie, or want to throttle down on the shot, choke up on the club. Or, if the lie is particularly worrisome, or the target tending to crowd you, it may be wiser to move on down to the No. 4 or No. 5 woods—or even an iron. Particularly where there is any doubt in your mind about jumping the ball up from a tight lie, or a divot mark, don't be ashamed to go to the 4-wood, or the 5-. It's far better to get the ball on its way, down the fairway, than to squirt it off into the Never-Never-Land.

The No. 4 wood is an easy club to hit with. So is the No. 5. Both have a lot of weight in the head and they swing well. They get a ball up quickly and can pop it out of real snug spots. Because the shafts are shorter than those of the driver and the other woods, you'll find yourself bending over the ball more than with the other woods. Your swing, consequently, tends to become more upright than with the longer clubs and, for some reason, this seems to make it much easier to hit the ball. Perhaps it's because, standing closer to the ball, you can see it better and you have more control over your swing.

The important change in the swing, however, as we move along down to the shorter woods, is that we're going to change our plan of attack. With the driver and No. 3 wood we were playing the ball directly off the left heel and sweeping it off the peg or the turf. Now we're going to shortstop the swing arc, so to speak, and move the ball back an inch or two so the club will meet it coming down into the base of the arc. It's almost as if we want to hammer the ball into the ground obliquely.

These shorter woods are divot takers. We're going to strike the ball a downward blow, squeeze it off the turf, then drive through—taking a feather of turf with the club. Incidentally, I've found that it's a good idea to choke down on the grip of these woods (except the driver) an inch to two inches. The shortened arc doesn't seem to lose me any distance, and it does seem to give me a substantially greater degree of control over the shot.

Although our swing plane is changing to a more upright one as we move down to the 4- and 5-woods, we still take the club back along an imaginary straight line from the ball to the hole, and bring it back along that same low, straight line. But we're not getting in behind the ball quite as much as we did with the driver. We're standing over the ball more and striking down on it.

The Irons

The importance of a good firm grip can't be overstated when we start discussing iron play. With the wood clubs, we have a certain margin for error. A weak grip will betray you at the top of the backswing—but so insidiously that you may not suspect it. But with the irons, and especially the long and medium irons, the flabby grip often results in the club-face turning on impact. This will effectively ruin your shot.

A second important consideration in dealing with the irons is this: Don't try to help the club. Don't lay the blade back and try to scoop the ball. Believe me, a lot of thought went into the development of the golf club and the designer set the angle of the blade to produce the type of shot expected of the club. He doesn't want any contribution from you. Just take your easy, full swing every time, finish high, and the rest will take care of itself.

Third, follow through on every shot. There are a couple of little shots, like the greenside "pop" shot, where we deliberately kill the swing right after we hit the ball. But we'll deal with these exceptions as we come to them. Generally speaking, on all iron shots your hands must finish higher on the follow-through than they were on the backswing.

Finally—and here we part company with a lot of traditional golf teaching—there's the matter of ball placement. The accepted theory is to continue moving the ball back toward the right toe as we move down the line from the long-range irons to the short ones. Theoretically, you wind up playing the 8- and 9-irons right off the right toe.

As I pointed out earlier, I don't believe in complicating the game, if possible. I like to keep things simple and I just don't see any point in making constant adjustments in the swing by moving the ball a distance of 14 to 16 inches. I do move the ball back slightly as I move along down into the shorter irons, but only far enough to compensate for the diminishing length of the shaft. This is a natural, and almost unconscious, adjustment.

After all, let's consider this matter for a moment. The idea, on all iron shots, is to hit *down* and *through,* taking turf *in front of the ball.* In other words, we expect to hit the ball a downward blow every time, striking it exactly in the same relative position every time and letting the angle of loft on the club-face do its job. This being the case, why should we keep moving the ball (and the bottom of the swing arc) backwards?

As we move from the long irons to the short ones, we're going to lose a few inches in shaft length, bringing us in closer to the ball and shortening the arc of the swing. These are the inches we have to compensate for in the placement of the ball. These are the inches which will bring the ball back to about, or slightly past, the center line between the feet.

Meanwhile, of course, the right foot is being drawn forward in creeping stages to complete the adjustment.

At least, this is my game, and I find it makes it possible for me to hit a golf ball always in exactly the same way, with the same swing.

THE LONG IRONS

As I pointed out back there on the first tee, the long irons are very difficult to hit for the weekend golfer. The face of the club is small. There is no mass there to support the half-missed shot. The "sweet spot" is elusive and the ball has to be hit perfectly or you come up empty. The No. 4 wood and the No. 1 iron have about the same degree of loft, and the No. 5 wood and No. 2 iron are matching clubs for loft and distance. Unless you have a very difficult lie, or unless you are trying to keep the ball low and boring into a wind, the shorter woods are much easier to handle and offer brighter promise of happier results.

For a truly atrocious lie, you're better off going all the way down to a medium-length iron and digging yourself out of the mess.

Let's forget about the No. 1 iron anyway. Nobody but a couple of pros with steel wrists ever use it. I much prefer the No. 4 wood and strongly recommend it to you as a way of life.

The No. 2 iron plays a little easier than the No. 1, but not much. To get anything out of it, you need a very good lie or a magnificent swing. Even then, you probably won't get the full distance you expect from the club. The 5-wood is a more reliable club and I recommend its use. Why complicate your life unnecessarily?

But if you feel you must play the 2-iron, choke down on it a couple of inches for better control. It's the same basic swing as you would use with the longer woods, but now you're standing closer to the ball and trying to hit down and through on the shot. You should take a small feather of turf after hitting the ball.

A common fault with this club is to press, going for maximum distance. This, of course, breaks the natural pace of the swing and frequently throws you off balance. Keep the swing lazy and fluid and bear in mind the hinge principle as applied to the wrists. Don't roll them. They should open and close squarely against the path of the swing, bringing the face of the club squarely into the ball with all the wrist support you can muster.

Don't try to give the ball additional lift with flicking wrists. Just whip the club through the impact zone and carry the hands through to a full finish, behind the left ear.

This instruction applies as well to the No. 3 iron, which is approximately the old mid-iron of yesteryear. With this club, however, we are beginning to move out of the wood club range and we are dealing with a club the high-handicap player can be expected to handle with a reasonable degree of competence. But again, any weakness in the grip will betray you. Because of the relatively small hitting area in the face of the club and the lack of supporting mass to carry the club through the shot firmly, the grip must be strong, the fingers acutely sensitive to the pressure requirements of the swing.

The 3-iron is struck with a square stance. We find ourselves standing a little closer to the ball now with a stance not quite as wide as for the woods. Let's play the ball back just about an inch behind the left heel and remember to draw the clubhead back low and square against the shot. Again, no rolling of the wrists. Everything square.

We should be nicely balanced on our heels and instep, sort of "sitting" to the shot. Whatever you do, don't crouch over the ball because the shortening shaft is bringing you in closer to it. This applies to all iron shots as we move along down into the medium-iron range.

Keep the right elbow in tight and push that left arm out as straight as your physical limitations will permit. Don't hurry the swing, and hit down on the ball, taking turf in front of it.

The No. 3 iron is a long gun. You're firing out with it and the temptation to press the club beyond its working distance has to be resisted. The best reminder of this is to remember to always choke down on the shaft. This makes a more upright swing virtually mandatory.

Now, as we move into the irons, we must be increasingly aware of the critical need to keep the left elbow from crumpling on impact. The left arm must be strong and extended right through the shot until the elbow is forced to bend as the hands carry the club up to a high finish.

THE MEDIUM IRONS

The middle irons—4-, 5- and 6-—bring us into the old mashie range and are not nearly as difficult to hit, although putting the ball where you want with them is something else again. Nevertheless, most Sunday golfers play these clubs and those in the short-iron range with a lot more confidence. This is because these clubs are full-faced, with a good "feel" to them, and usually are played to their full distance without any psychological inhibitions.

Now the ball is moving in still closer to you and you'll find it pretty hard to hit a sweeping shot, even if you want to. The swing is more upright and more compact in the sense that you feel you have firmer control over the execution of the shot. I think this is why the average golfer tends to develop an early and lasting confidence in these irons.

THE LONG IRON The long irons have an elusive "sweet spot" and are treachero
in the hands of a weekend golfer. Best of the lot for practical purpose is the No.
A strong grip is essential here—and, again, no rolling of the wrists. Stay square wi
the shot all the way and, whatever you do, *don't press.* You can't beat a long ir
into submission. Take it slow and easy and let the blade do what it's designed fc

With the reduction in the arc of the swing, we're going more and more now to a flat-footed stance. The left heel rises only slightly, not as conspicuously as it does to accommodate the more extended arc of the swing with the woods and longer irons.

One error to be avoided is the "yo-yo bob." Some players seem to suffer from a compulsion to compensate for the rooted left heel by straightening the right knee abruptly and rising on the back swing. The fact that the left heel remains planted shouldn't enter into your considerations at all. It's not a conscious positioning of the heel. Rather it is a consequence of the shortening swing arc and should develop quite naturally. The tempo and force of the swing don't change, remember? We take the club back and swing it through. The fact that the left heel now isn't rising from the ground as noticeably as before is simply a matter of some interest, not an end in itself.

Never press with these irons. If, for instance, you stand up to the ball with a 6-iron and there is a niggling doubt in your mind that you have enough club, step away. Return the club to the bag and go to the 5-iron. The danger here is one of lunging at the ball, shattering your timing and butchering the shot. You have to be swinging real good to hit a strong iron and still keep the ball straight.

As with all iron shots, play these with a firm grip and strong wrists. Hit down on the ball, which now is nearing the center line between the feet. With these clubs we want backspin because we're firing at the green and want to stop the ball. Hitting down and through, squeezing the ball off the turf, imparts this backspin.

On the backswing, carry the club back low and slow, square against the target always. The right wrist should hinge as the hands approach hip level. The club is carried up to a position just beyond vertical for the full shot, short of that for the soft or three-quarters shot.

These middle irons are commonly used for hitting the tee shot on the short par-3 holes. For some reason that

HE MEDIUM IRONS The medium irons are played with a somewhat more flat-
ooted stance because the shorter backswing doesn't require as much body pivot. But
eware of the "yo-yo" bob, caused by straightening the right knee (as if to compen-
te for the restricted pivot), followed by a lunging at the ball. Never press with these
ons. The tempo and force of the swing doesn't change at all.

escapes me completely, every book on golf instruction expresses horror at the idea of using a wooden peg for these tee shots. They argue that this isn't pure golf, and that iron shots should all be played off the turf. They urge the player to regard the shot as a fairway iron shot, to be set up on the turf accordingly. I don't understand this. I use a peg any time I can do it legally. Why not? It sets the ball up there where you can kiss it off neatly. Why make things any tougher than they are? One of the rewards of the game, and especially for the player of limited talent, is the satisfaction he gets from watching the soaring flight of an iron shot from the tee.

These medium irons are very popular also as chipping tools, although some pros prefer to go along down into the shorter irons for this work. I would recommend the 4-iron or 5-iron for chipping. Both clubs have enough loft to get the ball up over the thick grass of the apron, but aren't set back to a degree that they pose a problem involving a special delicacy of touch that only the full-time golfer acquires.

We won't go into the mechanics of the chip shot here. We'll discuss chipping and pitching in a separate section later. Hitting the wedge and the trap shot also will be discussed individually after a review of the short irons.

THE SHORT IRONS

With the 7-iron we're moving down into the short-range clubs. Again, these clubs are becoming progressively shorter in the shaft and wider and heavier in the face, with greater loft. Generally speaking, these clubs are easier to hit. But again, hitting the ball isn't enough when we draw the 7-, 8- and 9-irons. We're not concerned here with distance at all, but accuracy. Not only should we put the ball on the green with these clubs, but we should be firing at the pin.

We're hitting down on the ball and taking a pretty good scalp of turf in front of it with every shot. But the swing remains unchanged. The grip is the same and our position at

THE SHORT IRON The short irons are played solely for accuracy. Choke down on the shaft—to get closer to the ball itself—and never play one of these shots for its maximum distance. We are playing the ball closer to a point midway between the feet, to bring the blade into the ball on a descending arc, before it reaches the bottom of the arc, and take a fair scalp of turf *after striking the ball.*

the ball isn't altered—except that the ball is now midway between the feet, which are gradually being brought closer together.

With the 8-iron, we're getting right to the very heart of the short game and the ball should be taking a pretty good bite when it comes into the green. It ought to be "dancing" for us, as we say. That is, we're pinching it off the turf real good, and when it hits the green it should be digging in its heels for a short bounce and a kick-back.

We're choking down on the shaft a good 2 or 3 inches now with the 8- and 9-irons. It's not at all uncommon to see one of the tournament pros grip the 9-iron halfway down the shaft. These clubs are used quite often for chipping when you want to get the ball up and over an obstacle with a fast brake at the other end. It's a shot that calls for a lot of practice. The first few times, the ball will run. You have to get the feel of the shot. You have to be careful not to hit up, or "scoop," on the shot—and don't forget to follow through. Don't quit on impact. The temptation is great.

The feet are real close together now, with the weight evenly distributed. There should be more wrist action than with the longer irons, but the grip remains as firm as ever.

Actually, the 8- and 9-irons are used more often for pitching than for chipping. Feet are real close together, and the shot is played entirely with the hands and forearms. The body inclines over the ball, motionless. Two important things to remember on this shot: Take the club back slowly, and let the hands carry the clubhead through the shot easily and smoothly.

We'll discuss this shot, and the chip, at greater length in the next chapter, dealing with the short game.

3

The short game

The "Cone of Contention"

If you're a typical weekend golfer, your heartaches usually begin when you're 50 to 75 yards out from the green. This is the vale of tears, the "Valley of the Green Giant." I call it the "Cone of Contention" because within this cone, fanning out from the pin on an arc fronting the green, the tigers are separated from the rabbits. The guy with the sound short game pops it up there within the imaginary putting circle, while the confirmed loser is stubbing and flubbing his way to a 7 or an 8.

For the raw amateur, a carefully cultivated short game is tremendously important. These shots are critically important, in fact, if he hopes to play an interesting and competitive game. Why? Because the hard-bitten pro is usually home, on the green, with the same shot that carries the high-handicap player only within the "Cone of Contention."

In other words, this is where you measure out at least one stroke difference between you and me. I'm on the green at this point. You're 35 to 50 yards away. To play me anywhere near even you have to stick that next shot right at the pin for an easy putt while I'm taking my regulation two putts on the green.

But you're not going to be playing against a pro. You're playing Harry, Joe and Eddie, the guys who work down at the plant with you. All four of you are going to be out there in the "Valley of the Green Giant" and lying two. Now, if you can consistently get down in three from there—picking up your share of one-putt greens and par 3s as you go—you're going to score consistently in the low 80s or high 70s and stay ahead of Harry, Joe and Eddie on the balance sheet.

When you consider that about 75 per cent of your strokes are used up within 75 yards of the cup, the importance of refining your putting and short game becomes crushingly obvious. And there's no excuse for neglecting this phase of your game because it doesn't require a golf course for practice. You can refine your chipping stroke out in the yard, and you can develop a feel for the pitch-and-run over in the park.

But you have to work at it. You'll never find a nice, stroke-saving short game gift-wrapped under the Christmas tree. And Irving, down at the drugstore, doesn't dispense them in gelatin capsules. You have to get out there and swing the club, for hours, until the feel of these shots is burned indelibly into your muscle memory.

These are soft shots, or three-quarter shots, and have their own built-in dangers for the unwary golfer. There's something about an abbreviated swing that seems to drive the once-in-a-while player to spring at the ball, as if trying to compensate for the bobtailed swing. This, of course, completely destroys his timing and throws him off balance. In consequence, he lapses into the common error of throwing the clubhead at the ball, and quitting on the shot. He might just as well throw his hat at it.

Keep the Ball Running at the Pin

Before we even drop the first practice ball and line up a chip shot, let's give a little sober thought to the matter of developing an effective short game. I emphasize the word *effective*. In golf, that translates into low-scoring—because the idea is to get the ball into the hole. How you accomplish this—as long as it's done legally—is rather irrelevant. Style, without performance, is meaningless.

It's a funny thing, but the average American amateur golfer seems to be obsessed with the idea that every ball he hits into the green has to be loaded with backspin. This is one of the strangest misconceptions in the world of sport. I have two suspicions about it. Maybe it has grown out of watching the pros loft those rather long approach shots that have to bite and hold—or watch them pitch over greenside traps to a tight pin. In any event, the amateur golfer seems to have equated a lot of backspin with professional skill, and a mark of golfing distinction to strive for. True, it takes a degree of skill to make a ball spin in when it strikes the green. But every shot to the green doesn't necessarily call for this treatment.

My second suspicion about this style fad goes back to the ruling by the Royal & Ancient Society and the U.S.G.A. which outlawed deep scorings on the faces of clubs. It used to be the popular custom to file and chisel deep grooves in a club-face. These deep etchings enabled a skillful player to make the ball perform everything but a Seminole corn dance on the green. The two ruling bodies of golf put a stop to this and, subsequently, the frustrated golfers began working overtime to achieve maximum effect with legal tools. Putting backspin on the ball became, for quite a while, a special facet of the game that demanded long hours of polishing. Somehow, by the time this obsession filtered down to the rank-and-file golfers, it became almost a way of life.

There you have a couple of personal theories about this thing and you can take your choice, or reject both. The point

I want to make is this: You don't have to make every shot to the green a dancer. In fact, as long as you can safely keep the ball running at the pin, you're in scoring position. Don't ever forget that.

This means you don't have to be standing on the putting surface to reach for the putter. Believe me, from off the green I putt more often than I chip. Why? It's obvious that the putt is a much easier shot to make and you have a lot more control over the run of the ball. With the putter you're standing closer to the ball than with any other club. To borrow a phrase from Madison Avenue, you have "finger-tip control." Why be ashamed to play the easy shot? What are you trying to do out there—score, or put on a shot-making clinic for the other guys in your foursome?

Now, naturally, the conditions have to be right to play the "Texas wedge." To begin with, you have to be within 50 feet of the pin; that is, within range of the putting stroke. Beyond that, use of the putter is impractical because you're getting out of stroking range and into swinging range. And that's another shot entirely.

Secondly, you can't putt through thick grass. If there is a fringe of heavy grass between the ball and the green, you can forget about putting. The ball will have to be pitched over this fringe to the putting surface.

If the terrain fronting the green is extremely bumpy and uneven, or rain-sodden, an element of risk is introduced into your calculations and the use of the putt becomes a borderline decision. If you carefully consider these special conditions and still have confidence in your putter, by all means use it. The worst that can happen is that you will misjudge the run of the ball, or be carried wide of your target by the effect of the rough terrain.

But you will certainly reach the putting surface safely, in scoring range—by which I mean you should, in any event, be in position to have a go at the hole with your next putt.

Naturally, where there is any obstacle between you and the green which could influence the run of the ball, it should be chipped or pitched to the putting surface. Again, I would advise the high-handicap player (and even the weekend sharpshooter) to stop worrying about whether the ball bites or not. Use the 4-, 5- or 6-iron and play a pitch-and-run shot. It's so much easier to play and, with practice, easier to control.

Let's drop the ball off a typical green which is guarded by a rising slope and a fringe of chin whiskers between the fairway and the shaved surface. Now our problem is simply to leapfrog the ball over this fringe of heavy grass and the crest of the slope, and get it rolling to the hole.

Let's take the 5-iron here and choke down on it until the right hand is almost on the steel shaft. The stance is slightly open and the right elbow is almost resting against the right pocket. We should be resting comfortably, with our weight shaded to the right side. Our feet are rather close together, with the ball lying slightly behind the center-line. We're going to put a lot of wrist and forearm into this shot and we want to anchor the rest of the body except the knees, which act as swivel joints.

We bring the club straight back from the ball with the palm of the right hand and the back of the left hand remaining square against the hole all the way. This could almost be called an exaggerated putting stroke. There is little or no arc to the swing. The clubhead hugs the surface except at the very end of an extremely tight little backswing—and again at the very end of a loose and easy follow-through.

The ball will be struck with overspin. By calculating the length of our swing (which controls the force of the stroke), we'll just pop the ball over those fringe whiskers and drop it on the cut surface for a good roll at the pin.

The important thing to remember with this pitch-chip is to anchor the head just as you do with a putt (and, in theory, with every other shot). The greatest single enemy of this shot is a deplorable tendency to dip or bob the body in an attempt to give the ball a little added lift with a scooping action. Don't scoop. The blade of that 5-iron is set back at

an angle which will pick the ball up nicely and lay it down on the other side of the tall grass. All you have to do is bring the clubhead squarely into—and *through*—the shot. *Bump* the ball, don't scoop it.

As we back out to a distance of 20 or 30 yards, we are moving out of chipping range entirely and dealing exclusively with the pitching shots. Again, if the terrain is flat and firm and the green is wide open, we can stay with the less-lofted irons for a low-flying pitch that will give you a good run. It's the same shot as before except we extend the arc of our swing (abandoning the putting stroke entirely) for more distance.

Otherwise, the same guidelines apply—for stance, hand action and body discipline. Control of the ball's flight and subsequent run becomes an increasingly critical factor and only practice and application can sharpen your judgment.

As we move out from the pin, we'll move down the line to a more lofted club to raise the trajectory of the shot. Everyone should have in his bag of golf tricks a good pitch-and-run shot with the 7-iron or 8-iron. Too often I've seen amateur players automatically reach for the wedge when the situation screamed for a pitch shot. This American idolatry of the wedge goes back to the great national search for backspin. Don't misunderstand me. The wedge is a great club, perhaps the greatest addition to the golf bag in the last half-century. But there's a time and place for everything, and I'm convinced that the American golfer works the wedge to death.

I was reminded of this during the British Open championship at St. Andrews. That magnificent links is one of the most intriguing tests of golf I've ever encountered, and nothing at all like the typical American parkland course. For reasons that are both economic and traditional, our British cousins don't go in for heavily watered greens and fairways. This means the wedge shot, the darling of American pro and amateur alike, is relatively ineffective over there. You can throw a shot up on those greens at St. Andrews

THE PITCH-AND-RUN The pitch-and-run is the heart and soul of the short game, the stroke-saver that separates the players from the lower orders of vertebrates. This is a judgment shot that calls for a sensitive touch, an air-conditioned nervous system—and lots of backyard practice. It's the shot that keeps the ball "running at the pin," as we say.

with lots of bite on it, but when the putting surface is like granite it doesn't offer anything to bite.

On those fast fairways and rock-hard greens I choked up on those 7- and 8-irons and let the ball run up there.

The Wedge Shot

The wedge, with its heavy flanged sole, is an American invention, developed originally as a sand iron by Gene Sarazen. You might call it a by-product of failure. As Gene tells it, he made the first wedge because he was throwing away too many shots in the traps. So he took his niblick and soldered globs of lead along the sole until he had a club with an exceptionally heavy, wide flange that would act like an aileron on an airplane—driving the face of the club up and out of the sand instead of digging in deeper.

At the same time, Sarazen was looking for a club that would drive the ball *up* when he hit *down* on it. The upshot of all this puttering around in the machine shop was the wedge, the grand old stroke-saver. I don't know what life was like before the wedge turned up in the golf bag. It must have been grim.

Mind you, I have just finished cautioning against the *wrong* use of the wedge. But there is a time and a place when the wedge is the only club for the shot.

The wedge, as I said, was designed as a sand iron. A later modification, with the same deep set-back of the blade, but with a less formidable flange on the sole, was developed as a "pitching" wedge. The two are often used interchangeably today and, since there is room in the bag for only one of these special purpose irons, it becomes a matter of taste. How heavy a flange do you want? For all practical purposes, a wedge is a wedge—and we'll deal with it as a one-design club.

I don't have a favorite club. A working professional can't have a favorite club. This is a bad amateur habit and

THE CHIP SHOT The chip shot is really nothing but an exaggerated putt with lofted iron. Choke down on the 5-, 6-, or 7-iron until the hands are almost on t steel shaft, if you like. Many pros like to get down within putting elevation of t ball. Shade your weight to the right side and hold right elbow snug against sid Bring the club straight back from the ball, with the right palm and back of left ha square against the hole. It's a tight little backswing with a loose, easy follow-throug

leads to the development of a distorted and one-sided game, built around a couple of master clubs. Beware of the trap. Still and all, if there's one club in the bag I have a rather special affection for, I'd have to reach for the wedge. They tell me I use it well and, I suppose, this is the reason.

The wedge rapidly outgrew its original purpose, as a sand iron. It was such a perfect club for lofting the ball and dropping it almost vertically at the pin that it swiftly was adapted to lobbing the ball over those very traps it was designed to escape in the original Sarazen model. Then it became a natural for slashing the ball out of rough, and for salvaging those glimmering pars from bad lies.

Basically, the club is used for hitting into the green from any distance up to 100 yards, occasionally farther, when you need a high trajectory to clear an obstacle and drop the ball down abruptly on the pin. The club is never swung with full power. It is essentially a soft shot, played with a three-quarter swing or less. So, you can see, it's a delicate shot, to be played with finesse that comes only after hours and hours of practice.

With the wedge, the idea is to get the ball up in the air quickly and stop it quickly when it lands. We play the shot from a slightly open stance, the ball just forward of the center-line. If we want to stop the ball dead, we open the face of the club slightly. We'll close it somewhat if we want the ball to roll when it lands. For accuracy, we always remember to keep the back of the left hand squarely facing the hole, and the swing is "square back, square through." We always hit down and through.

The wedge is a very versatile club, which may help to explain its blind popularity with so many golfers. It can be used for a whole bagful of shots, many of them being played with the wrong club.

But let's consider some hypothetical wedge shots where this is clearly the club for the job. Let's assume we're lying some 10 to 15 yards from the green with a yawning sand trap between us and the putting surface. The ball has to get

THE WEDGE SHOT The wedge is played from a rather open stance with the ball shaded back toward the right foot. The club is never swung with full power and, as often as not, is "punched"—that is, played by opening the blade for a fast stop and cocking the wrists immediately as the club is started back, so the hands come into the shot ahead of the blade in a "chopping" motion.

THE CONFIDENCE GAME The sand shot needs confidence and practice—and practice will bring confidence. The ball is carried out of its bed on a cushion of sand. Experience will help you to handle various textures of sand, wet and dry. You must play the shot firmly, with an unhurried swing, and carry through to a high finish. Never quit on this shot!

up quickly in a high, short trajectory to drop just beyond the trap for a brief run at the pin.

We use a short punch shot, opening up the face for a quick stop at touch-down. We break the wrists almost immediately as we start the club back, keeping the hands well ahead of the club. The last thing we want to do in a situation like this is to hit the ball "fat" and dump it into the sand. If we do, it's six-five-and-even that the ball will bury itself and then we'll have a brand new problem—as if things weren't bad enough.

So we come back into the shot with the hands still ahead of the club. We drop the club down and into the ball rather abruptly with almost a chopping motion, except that instead of stopping the club as you would an axe, we swing through with firm wrists and a strong, positive wrist action. With practice and confidence, this shot will hold no terrors for you and, in fact, you'll almost welcome the prospect of popping the ball over a trap as an exercise in skill.

Let's take another case. Perhaps we're lying just off the green and in a pretty nasty lie. The pin is well back on a hard, sun-baked green. Here's a case where the pitch-and-run shot is loaded with risk. The conditions call for a "drag" shot. We want to dig the ball out of its cuppy lie and get it running at the hole.

This is a short wedge shot. We choke 'way down on the shaft until the right hand is flirting with the steel shaft again. Now we're going to crowd the ball, playing it somewhat back toward the right foot. Not too much. Just enough to bring the club-face into the shot before it reaches the bottom of its natural swing arc.

Again, a short, firm backswing, cocking the wrists immediately so the hands will be moving ahead of the club. The back of the left hand is square to the hole, as always, and it leads us into the shot as we hit down and through. If we put everything together, the ball will land, take a couple of jumps, and skid up to the hole like one of those movie cartoons that show a guy sliding forward while his feet are pumping like crazy to brake his forward motion.

Here's another hypothetical instance which calls for the wedge, or sand iron. Frequently you may find yourself pitching back to a green that slopes away from you. A pitch-and-run shot could go galloping off like a runaway. What we hope to accomplish here (assuming the conditions rule out the use of the putter) is to loft the ball into a high trajectory and drop it steeply on the green with lots of backspin for a dead stop, or very short roll.

This is a tricky and dangerous shot. Unless you're very accomplished with that wedge I would strongly urge that you look for another avenue of approach. The margin for error in a shot like this is shaved too thin for comfort. If there's any way to roll it up there, go that route.

A final word of summary on the use of the wedge:

Bear in mind, the wedge is designed for a special purpose —to get a ball into orbit quickly and drop it vertically, with backspin, or "brakes." For this purpose it's an ideal tool. Perfect yourself in the use of it. It will save you many, many strokes.

But don't use the wedge indiscriminately just because the shot that comes off its blade is such a beautiful thing to watch. You're not out there on the course to star in a motion picture. I presume you're out there to negotiate the course in the fewest possible number of strokes. So look the situation over. If the circumstances call for the high loft and the quick stop (an obstacle between you and the green and a tight pin on the other side), by all means use the wedge. But, if the green is wide open, the terrain smooth and firm, and the green offers plenty of running room to the hole, take my advice and run that ball in there with a medium iron or even the putter.

The Nearing of the Green

For the professional golfer, the second shot he hits on every hole is the critical one. In every case, the purpose of the tee shot is to put him in position to play his second. In

THE EXPLOSION The sand wedge is designed on the principle of the aileron. The broad flange on the sole of the club provides a planing surface that prevents the club from digging its own grave in the sand. Instead, it planes through the loose grains and rides upward as it passes beneath the embedded ball.

HILLSIDE LIES From an uphill lie, there is a tendency to hook, or pull, the ball. Compensate by opening the face of the club and playing wide of the target. Use a more straight-faced club than otherwise because your position, in relation to the slope, subtly changes the loft of the blade or clubface. The downhill lie reverses these factors. Adjust accordingly.

most instances, this second shot brings him into the green for that agonizing, soul-searing experience called putting.

On the other hand, the high-handicap amateur rarely gets home in two. That's why he's a 90 shooter. His second shot brings him into what I call the "Cone of Contention"— within a 30- to 40-yard radius of the hole. From here on in, it becomes a question of whether the weekend golfer is going to get down in three or four strokes—for a bogey or a double bogey.

Is this your game? I'll lay even money it is. So, what happens? You and Charley play every weekend. You both play the same game. The one who gets his bogey with greater regularity wins the dollar Nassau and you buy the beers.

Then, one day, you meet a guy on the first tee who joins you. He has the same hitch in his swing that you have and the three of you are a good match—except for one thing. This stranger has a peculiar knack of throwing that ball up close to the pin every time, and he runs in four or five of those 8-foot putts during the round. Your 88 is two strokes better than Charley's 90 for the day—but Angus, here, comes in with an 84 and he's drinking on you guys.

I can just about guarantee anyone reading this book that he can cut four or five strokes off his handicap if he wants to get out there and work on his short game. It takes a lot of self-discipline and this is something the average weekend golfer lacks. Nor do I condemn him for it. After all, if the game is a form of recreation for him, he doesn't want to work at it.

Still, if he persists in playing, he would be less than human not to want to play up to his maximum potential. So there he is, draped on the horns of his private dilemma. He insists on playing the game. He wants to play it well. *Ergo:* He must find the time and the patience to work at it.

The reason I hammer so hard on this subject of developing a good short game is that pitching and chipping are shots that can be practiced in the corner of any playground, park or schoolyard. It's only a question of setting aside the required practice time, knowing what you're trying to accomplish and working for perfection.

We have talked here of the common shots the player will encounter as he zeroes in on the green. There are also a few uncommon shots that deserve passing mention. In many cases, it's foolhardy to attempt them. They are loaded with danger. And the tyro golfer will do well to bear in mind my earlier counsel to try and keep that ball rolling toward the hole—well out of trouble.

But there are unusual circumstances that come readily to mind and it's interesting, from a clinical point of view, to consider them.

For instance, frequently you'll face a plateau green that is guarded by a mound, or running ridge that is like a junior-size bunker. The conditions rule out a running shot, and you have a choice of lofting the ball over this guardian mound or drilling it into the side of the slope to carom it over the ridge for a run at the hole. This is a difficult shot to play, requiring lots of practice and judgment.

I'm reminded rather sharply of this type of shot by an incident that occurred during the Thunderbird Open tournament at Westchester, New York. I was playing with Mike Souchak and went into a par-3 hole with a two-stroke lead over him. But my tee shot left me wide of the green and lying behind one of these ridges, and I elected to bounce my next shot over the hill. I took my 8-iron and swung, but I hit the shot too hard and the ball carried over the hill and ran to the far side of the green where it stopped, luckily.

Nevertheless, I then three-putted—and lost three strokes to Souchak. Now I was one down and the whole complexion of the round was changed by one risky shot that didn't come off. That's why I strongly recommend against attempting the difficult shot when there is a simple, safe solution to the problem.

Another shot you'll encounter that deserves some special consideration is the pop shot. This, by the way, is the only shot you'll ever play without a follow-through and—with the exception of the drag shot—the only one in which the hands are in front of the club all the way.

The pop shot is used when you find yourself in thick, matted grass or rough, close to the green. You'll notice, sometimes, a heavy growth of rough around the green and this is tough stuff to contend with. If you know how to play from it, you're that much ahead of the game. But it takes know-how and practice.

In some respects it is very similar to the cut shot. We open the blade and take the club back along the outside-in track because we're going to come back along the same track and slice across the ball. Actually, in playing the pop shot, we hit behind the ball—hitting grass and ball together. The shot is played with an open stance and lots of wrist action, "throwing" the blade in behind the ball. When hit correctly, the ball will pop out of the grass without any spin, or very little forward roll.

This is a phase of the game, by the way, in which the ladies show a special aptitude. When it comes to snaking a ball into the cup from The Valley, I can assure you the female of the species is far more deadly than the male. And the reason is fairly obvious. The girls (I'm happy to report, in case you haven't been paying too much attention to them lately) don't have the muscular development to match the male golfer's power. So they concentrate on the finesse shots. I believe, too, the ladies have a natural, feminine delicacy of touch which is critically important in refining the short game.

A few years back there was an excellent woman golfer in North Carolina named Estelle Lawson Page. She was almost a perennial winner of the Women's North & South championship and ventured out of her home state once to win the U.S.G.A. Women's Amateur title. Although I never saw her play, they tell me she had an almost uncanny knack for getting down in two from off the green.

About a dozen years ago, my business manager, Fred Corcoran, took a team of American women pros to England, challenged a team of crack British male amateurs, and skunked them. Once our little ladies reached the "Valley of the Green Giant," it was Katy-bar-the-door. The girls were flipping the ball up there from all angles and bowling in those putts like machines.

All of which confirms my belief that developing an effective short game is a matter of "sensory perception," to borrow a fraction of a phrase popularized by Professor Rhine of Duke. Chipping and pitching are, in a sense, "finger shots" —much like putting. They call for a high degree of sensitivity in the fingers, which hold and, in a large measure, control the action of the golf club.

I point this out by way of reminder that the golf grip is a "finger grip." You can't get a good shave wearing boxing gloves, and you'll never shave your handicap clutching a golf club in your sweaty hams. Check your grip. Check the delicate balance of the club against those pressure points we discussed in the last chapter. Then work with those chipping tools in the backyard until they come alive in your hands and you begin hitting those shots with a touch that is almost a caress.

In summary, then, the short game consists of three types of basic shots: the chip, the pitch-and-run and the pitch-and-stop. I would strongly urge anyone to build his short game around the pitch-and-run concept. Reserve the loft-and-stop shots with the 9-iron and wedge for the specific conditions that call for them. These high, arching shots are used to lob a ball *over* danger—whether it's a trap, a pond, rough and brush or treacherous terrain—and drop it steeply onto the green.

Don't be ashamed to use your putter off the green. Remember, the chip shot is basically an extended putt, played with an exaggerated putting stroke. Why not use the tool best adapted to the shot?

If you do choose to throw the ball up there with the wedge, however, I suggest you aim at the top of the flag, not the hole. There is a tendency among Saturday afternoon golfers to come up short on the shot. If you aim for the top of the pin, you cancel out this natural weakness.

And never go all-out on a wedge shot. If you have to power a wedge shot, you've got the wrong club in your hands. The wedge is rarely pressed beyond 50 per cent of its potential length.

Remember, too, that these are all finesse shots, not muscle shots. Choke down on the club. The closer you are to the ball, the clearer you can see what you're doing and the better control you will have over the shot because you are reducing the arc of your swing.

Finally, if you can consistently put that ball up there inside an imaginary 20-foot circle from any spot 25 yards from the green, you can play an interesting and competitive game with anyone.

4

Putting: the other game

The object of this game is to put the ball into a hole which has a diameter of 4¼ inches. The rest is prologue, just a cross-country wild goose chase in search of a climax. This ultimate stroke, the one that ends all discussion, is the putt.

I rather suspect that more words have been written on the subject of putting, and more wild theories concocted, than on any other phase of the game. The reason is obvious. As Ben Hogan put it, there is no similarity between golf and putting; they are two different games—one played in the air, and the other on the ground. You have to be a good putter to be a good golfer, but you don't necessarily have to be a good golfer to be a good putter. If you could assemble the entire population of the United States for a national open putting championship, the winner would probably turn out to be somebody named Artemus Snaggle, of East Windbreak, Nevada. Runner-up would probably be an eleven-year-old child—and a girl, at that!

They tell me Walter Winchell couldn't break 150 on a regulation golf course, but was a genius with a putter in his hand. Most of the pros concede that the world's greatest putter is George Lowe, a delightful fellow who gave up the arduous grind of tournament golf to assume the role of the world's guest. George continues to follow the tour, living handsomely on the overflow from the horn of plenty and venturing as far as the practice putting green on occasion to give a costly lesson in putting.

Considering how irrelevant the putting stroke is in any earnest study of golfing technique, it's ironical that this narrow part of the game should account for about one-half your strokes! Yet, this is the case. Two putts is the standard for every hole, accounting for 36 of the strokes Colonel Bogey is supposed to expend on a regulation par-72 course.

The depressing part of it is, there isn't much fat to be trimmed from this part of the game, either. At best, we can hope to refine our putting technique so we can reasonably hope to negotiate an eighteen-hole round without three-putting any greens—and possibly win back a stroke or two from par with a couple of well-aimed runners that duck into the hole on the first charge.

I think any discussion of putting technique must deal first with the putting stroke, or the physical act of striking the ball, and then, in turn, with such matters as gauging distance and direction. There's no point in discussing putting styles. You grope around, shuffle and re-shuffle your feet, and bend and twist and writhe until you find a putting stance that feels comfortable, and a manner of hitting the ball that makes sense—at least, to you. I've seen some putting styles that look like they came off a drawing board at the Disney studios. But the originator has the last laugh if he can make the ball pop into the hole out of this ridiculous crouch.

How you grip a club is entirely up to you. You can hold it like a broom, if it suits you. Most players use the same overlapping grip they employ with the other clubs. I use the

THE PUTT Style means nothing in putting, as long as you can put the ball in the hole. Basic rules to remember: (1) Keep the head still; (2) Hit the shot with the right hand; and (3) Guide the stroke with the left hand by keeping the back of that hand square against the hole all the way.

"reverse overlapping" grip. Instead of curling the little finger of the right hand over the left index finger, I take a full grip with the right hand and curl the left index finger over the little finger of the right hand. I do this because I'm satisfied the putt is strictly a right-hand stroke, as we'll see in just a moment.

Some completely reverse the hand positions, placing the left hand below the right hand on the shaft and sort of backhanding the ball with a stroke that is basically a sweeping motion. As I say, this is a personal thing, this putting grip. Because mental poise and equanimity account for some 90 per cent of putting success, the important thing is to feel comfortable and relaxed when you bend over the putt.

Generally speaking, there are certain fundamental elements which apply broadly to most successful putting games. Most pros stand squarely at the ball and play it dead center, directly under the head. At least I do, and this goes for most of the top tournament players. The feet are placed at right angles with the hole, at "twelve o'clock high."

The putt is essentially a hand-and-forearm shot, played with no body movement. The wrists are the hinges and the club is swung like a pendulum. The hands are in close to the body now, and the right elbow is tucked against the right side because we want to limit all movement to the hands and wrists. The club is brought straight back from the ball and returned to the shot along the same low, flat plane. The blade doesn't open at all. There is no need for it to. The backswing should measure only 10 to 12 inches at the most.

The putt is struck with the right hand. It is the only golf shot that actually is *struck,* in the sense that there is a positive and conscious act of *striking.* From tee to green we don't really hit the ball in that sense; we swing the club and let the clubhead strike the ball. Now, with the putter, we're not swinging the club. We're actually *hitting* the ball with the blade of the club.

So the left hand is subordinated. Indirectly, it serves as a control, leading the stroke through and toward the hole.

I say "indirectly" because it's the left arm which usually does the actual leading, not the hand. A popular form, fancied by the late Horton Smith, who was one of the greatest putters the game ever knew, is to point the left elbow directly at the hole so the left arm, leading the hands into the shot, will carry them right along the line to the hole.

A third element in the putting stroke is *overspin*. The idea is to set the ball in motion toward the hole—and keep it rolling until it gets there. So we strike the ball an upward blow with the club, coming into the shot as the blade passes the bottom of its arc and starts to rise. This will impart an overspin which is so desirable. Nothing is so infuriating as the putt that limps up to the hole and dies a few inches short of the lip. If you're hitting your putts with good overspin, you'll find a lot more of them rolling boldly up the front walk and demanding entrance instead of expiring weakly on the doorstep.

A "drag" putt is one that is struck a downward blow to give it backspin. Some players use this stroke to slide the ball at the hole on a downhill putt—or to prevent a well-struck putt from popping in and out of the hole, or lipping or rimming the cup. I wouldn't recommend that you fool around with it. If you miss a downhill putt, you're in trouble anyway. The other arguments for this stroke leave me blank. I just don't dig them.

The fourth and final fundamental element in the putting stroke is consistent with the rest of the game. The head must not come up to follow the track of the ball. Keep your head down all the way and listen for the putt to drop. You'll know when it does, even if you don't hear it. Your opponent will offer some complimentary remark, like "Oh, you lucky bum!"

The other two aspects of putting—distance and direction—share equal ranking. Control of either means nothing without the other. Nevertheless, I'm inclined to lend a shade more importance to the matter of gauging distance. Most of your three-putt greens can be blamed on a feeble approach putt from the Outer Mongolia of the putting surface. Most faulty approach putts are errors of distance rather than errors of direction. Or, to put it another way, rarely does a long positioning putt wander more than a foot off-line either side of the hole. But so many of these heroic stabs fall yards short of the target—or go galloping yards beyond it.

Sticking a long putt close enough to the pin to ensure the second one depends to a large extent on an innate ability to gauge distance and to respond with the required putting stroke. But the fine art of putting is a compendium of gimmicks, psychological crutches and mental sleight-of-hand. Any one or several of these stunts can be useful if they serve their purpose: a dose of adrenalin for the confidence gland.

Lloyd Mangrum, one of the greatest players of our time, used a little mental brace of sorts. He imagined the hole was in the center of a 3-foot circle and he stroked the ball to enter that circle. By enlarging his target zone to proportions that his mind could accept and deal with realistically, Lloyd was able to put those long putts awfully close to the pin— and he sank his share of them. Mangrum was a deadly putter, with the cool aplomb of a burglar.

Here's another one, for the mathematics student:

I know a guy who is murder with those long runners. He says he doesn't putt for the pin at all. He picks a spot midway, gauges the force needed to get the ball there, does some fast mental arithmetic and doubles the force factor. By hitting the ball twice as hard as he figures he would have to to get halfway to the hole, he cozeys the ball up there real nice-like.

My advice to the weekend warrior is to bang the ball boldly. The natural tendency is to err on the rabbit side and fall well short of the hole. So, give the ball that extra thump and don't worry about over-running the cup. You can always putt back again. And, who knows? A few of those bold ones might hang on line and jump in. But you'll never, never sink a putt that curls up and goes to sleep 10 feet short of the hole.

Before you go to the first tee, and as you wind up your warm-up session on the practice green, practice putting for distance. Don't worry about accuracy. The putts you'll be facing out on the course won't bear any resemblance to those on the practice green—except in one important detail: One foot will still measure 12 inches, regardless of which green you're on.

The grain and condition of the green, of course, will have an important influence on the roll of the ball. By all means, learn to read a green but, for Heaven's sake, don't become a graduate student in agronomy! This is a game, remember? Don't drive the rest of your foursome insane while you set up a transit and go into a civil engineering trance. You can read a green at a glance, for all practical purposes.

The blades lie one way or another, and the ball will be guided to a limited degree by the direction of these blades. On a sunny day the grain will be shiny if the grain is with you, dark if it's against you. Against the grain you have to strike the ball a little harder. With the grain, the ball will tend to maintain its forward momentum a little longer. That's all there is to it. If the grain and slope run in opposite directions, they'll cancel each other out.

Wet grass, naturally, will slow the ball, so allowance must be made for a heavy green. Conversely, a sun-baked and wind-swept green, lightly watered, usually plays lightning fast and you have my sympathy—especially if you're faced with a downhill sidehill putt!

Speaking of sidehill putts, the good putter masters the knack of playing the rolling contours. A putt which has to traverse a sidehill slope must be started along an arc which will nullify the drag of gravity. This additional slope which the ball covers on its way from the club to the hole is called "borrow," and it's a pretty good general rule on this type of putt to allow more "borrow" than you think you should. Again, we have a situation where the tendency is to err on the rabbit side and fail to start the ball high enough on the slope.

The pull of gravity increases proportionately as the putt begins to lose its momentum. It begins to fade downhill slowly at first, then with a sharply increasing angle of decline. It's like a stone that you throw which follows a fairly constant arc for the rising trajectory, then falls rapidly until it is dropping vertically.

Like so many aspects of putting, this judgment of borrow is an art that has to be developed and refined through practice and experience.

I can't leave the subject of distance without one final comment. The object of this game, as I pointed out in my tee shot on this chapter, is to put the ball in the hole. Not *near* the hole, mind you, but *in* the hole. I know you're a nice guy and I know you play with nice guys. We're all a bunch of nice guys out there on the course. But nice guys observe the Rules of Golf as laid down by the United States Golf Association. One of the worst habits you can fall into is that of conceding yourself the final putt. I love these guys who reach out and sweep the ball in the general direction of the hole, pounce on it and announce, "Give me a five." I'll give him a five when he lines the ball up and putts it into the cup. And I want to see you do the same. That's the way the game is played—winter and summer, Sundays and Thursdays.

Turning now to the matter of direction:

You're on your own here. This subject goes right down deep into the marrow of the brain. Or perhaps it's some other deep recess of the human anatomy. In any event, you either have a sense of direction, or you don't. I know some guys who have the unerring instinct of a homing pigeon. Others couldn't putt a ball into the crater at Vesuvius from a distance of 3 feet. Why? ¿*Quién sabe, amigo?* Maybe it's written in the stars.

The otherwise simple act of hitting a ball into a hole is complicated by the fact that, unless the hole is close enough to be included in your peripheral vision, you can't see your target. Instead, you study the line between the ball and the hole, try to freeze a mental picture of this putting path, then stand up to the ball and stroke it. This is an act of concentration. The success or failure of the putt usually depends on how faithful to fact that mental picture remains.

To overcome this natural handicap most good putters select a target point lying within their peripheral range of vision as they stand over the putt—a distinctive blade of grass or a tiny area of discoloration on the surface which lies directly along the route to the hole. They putt to roll the ball over this immediate target to put the ball along the desired track to the cup. It's practical strategy.

If you're lying within 3 or 4 feet of the hole, don't worry about the contour of the green. Just bang the ball firmly at the cup. In that limited distance, the subtle slopes you'll encounter aren't going to influence the direction of a well-hit putt. Play it straightaway.

A few paragraphs ago we mentioned the fact that, among the fundamental principles of putting, one calls for the right hand to hit the putt and the left arm to point the way. Now that we're dealing with direction, let's return to that for a moment.

In the popular putting stance, the left arm is set at an awkward and unnatural angle. While the elbow points at the hole, the left wrist is set squarely against the target. The effect is the same as if you were to crouch over a putt with your left elbow pointing at the pin, then flip your hand over so the back of it is facing down toward the ground. Now, break your wrist back as if it were hinged, and the back of your hand is facing the hole.

This is the position of the hand as it leads the putter through the stroke. It should continue out towards the hole on the same plane, with the back of the hand squarely facing the cup. This is the commonly accepted method of steering a putt in the right direction and insuring that it will continue to travel the prescribed line.

A final note on putting. I'm reminded of Sarazen's oft-quoted advice: Miss 'em quick. The tournament professionals are very deliberate about lining up a putt. They survey it carefully from all angles and minutely scrutinize the putting surface. Some are by nature slow and deliberate. For some, this ballet on the green masks an inner struggle as they compose themselves and concentrate intensely on the shot. With so much money riding on the outcome of each putt and his very livelihood at stake, the pro is entitled to deal with a putt in his own way and in his own good time.

Unfortunately, the widespread exposure of the pro game on television has attracted a vast army of disciples among the weekend golfers who mistakenly ape these mannerisms under the impression that it will improve their game. This is mistaking the form for the substance. Fiddling around with putts, stalking from one end of the green to the other and squatting on your heels to sight in a putt really don't do a thing for you. All they do is clutter up the golf course with fuming foursomes behind you and take a lot of the fun out of the game.

There's some psychological stalling involved here, too. There are people who hate to make decisions. I suppose you can't expect them to change personalities on the golf course. But I'd like to point out to them that they have to hit the putt, sooner or later, and the sooner they go at it the better their chances are. Concentration is a fleeting thing at best, measured in seconds.

The best putters are the confident putters, and a confident putter doesn't drift off into a state of suspended animation. He goes about the job efficiently, neither hurrying the shot nor dawdling over it. It's a course I earnestly recommend in the interests of faster play and better golf.

I can't emphasize too strongly this matter of confidence. I believe, too, that it's all entwined with the personality. From observation, I've come to the conclusion that the best putters in the game are the breezy and optimistic people. In contrast, poor putters seem to be cranky and cantankerous characters. I don't know; perhaps missing a lot of putts makes them cranky. Still and all, you show me a good putter and I'll show you a fellow with a cheerful and buoyant attitude toward life.

I know from experience that confidence is the key to an effective putting technique. Back there in 1961, my golfing fortunes were at their lowest ebb. I couldn't buy a putt and, in consequence, the rest of my game was suffering. I was just playing out the string and very seriously considering chucking it all. In fact, I was heading for the Buick Open that year with the firm intention of calling it a career after that and heading back to California to look for a job—any kind of a job.

But there I was in Detroit and, on the impulse, I picked up the telephone and called Horton Smith. I had met Horton casually a couple of years before and I knew his immense reputation as a putter. I told him my troubles and asked him if he could spare an hour or two for a lesson. He was most gracious.

"You've just lost your confidence, Tony," he said. "Come along over and I think we can work it out."

So that day, for nearly two hours, Horton worked with me. He did most of the putting and most of the talking. I just listened, watching him putt and, from time to time, hitting a few. It was the greatest hour or two I ever spent in my life and an experience I can never forget. It was a Dutch uncle session and I came away from it with a completely new attitude, a fresh shot of confidence. It was a turning point in my game and in my golfing career.

Smith convinced me that day of something I already firmly believed—that putting is a right-hand stroke. That is why I use the reverse overlapping grip. Horton agreed 100 per cent. He gave me a little exercise that day which he said would hone my putting touch. He told me to take the putter in my right hand and throw down three balls. Then, using only the right hand, putt one ball from 4 feet out, the second from 5 feet away and the third from about 6 feet. I've used this little five-finger exercise ever since as a prelude to serious putting practice.

My debt to Horton Smith goes beyond an invaluable putting lesson that day in Detroit. I am the richer for a few memories of him. I recall vividly my match with Peter Alliss in the Ryder Cup competition when Alliss had me dormie—

two down and two to play. I took the 17th with a birdie, but I was trapped at the 18th and Peter was over the green.

He chipped out about 15 feet short and missed the putt. I blasted out about 5 feet short and, as I knelt to sight the line on the putt, I looked beyond the hole and saw Horton in the gallery, watching me gravely. His eyes were talking to me and I got the message, clear and strong. I took my stance, locked my head in position and banged the ball into the cup to halve the match.

As I walked off the green, Horton greeted me and smiled broadly.

"It couldn't go any place else, could it?" he said.

I just don't know what makes a good putter or a bad putter. Stance and style, apparently, have nothing to do with it. Billy Casper, for instance, stands with his feet close together. Arnold Palmer locks himself into position with that peculiar knees-akimbo stance. Gary Player and Jack Nicklaus choke 'way down on their putters to get close to the ball. So there is no right or wrong technique. I do know this, though: I've seen rotten putters become good putters by hard work—just by putting thousands of balls into the hole in practice. This form of devotion to work has to pay off. It isn't a drill that everyone can undertake.

There is no secret to putting. The best advice I can offer is to build confidence in yourself and your ability to run that ball into the hole. And always give it a good run at the cup. The hole is there, waiting. It's large enough to take the ball. All you have to do is give it a chance to go in. That's the closest thing there is to a putting secret.

5

Nobody knows the trouble I've seen

This vexing game, as I pointed out somewhere back along the fairway, is an eighteen-hole flirtation with disaster. I think it's only fitting that Scotland, which gave the world golf, also furnished a suitable poet laureat in Bobbie Burns, who wrote, "The well-laid plans of mice and men gang aft agley." That goes for well-planned golf shots, too.

However carefully you plot your course from tee to green, the journey is fraught with peril. Inevitably, you're going to find yourself roaming the back country or marooned on the beach of a sand trap. When this happens, as it's bound to, you are faced with the ultimate golfing test: How to escape with only minor bruises on your score card.

Before we start running through a catalog of trouble shots, let me say there *is* such a thing as an unplayable lie. And there *is* such a thing as an unplayable shot. It's a smart golfer who recognizes both. Believe me, I've seen the rawest of raw amateurs tackle utterly impossible shots that no professional would even consider. Needless to say, they never bring it off. Things invariably go from bad to worse. Panic gives way to despair and, before you know it, a par-5 disaster that might have been salvaged with a 6 or a 7 becomes one of those ghastly 10s.

An unplayable lie is one that offers no chance of a successful shot. You are the sole judge of this. When your ball winds up in this position, there's nothing to do but take your one-stroke penalty and drop the ball out where you can get at it.

In passing, let me suggest also that you know your rules. Bear in mind that the rules offer you relief from certain unnatural hazards as occasional water and ground under repair, random pieces of maintenance equipment and assorted pieces of flotsam and jetsam that don't belong on any properly supervised golf course. You may lift without penalty from these situations and you owe it to yourself and your game to understand these circumstances.

While the rule book provides for the unplayable lie, it says nothing about the unplayable shot—and here's where the Sunday golfer gets hurt. One of the conspicuous differences between the professional and the high-handicap amateur is the fact that the professional never gambles unless the stakes are high and the reward justifies the risk. This is a judgment thing. You calculate your chances and weigh these chances against the certain penalty of failure. Then you make your decision. Rarely is the risk warranted.

For instance, when you're boxed in by trees, with only the narrowest kind of an opening for recovery, it's time to give some serious consideration to surrendering a stroke and chipping safely back to playing position. If your only shot requires perfection, leaving absolutely no margin for error, common sense should scream at you: "No! No! That shot's not for you or you wouldn't be in this predicament in the first place!"

Yet, there are bullheaded players of limited talent who wander off into the woods every Saturday and sound like they're writing a symphony for drums. These woodpeckers persistently throw away three or four strokes playing carom shots off the maples when an easy chip shot would put them back in safe playing position at a cost of only one stroke.

One of the cardinal rules for scoring in this game is: The best way to get out of trouble is to *stay* out of trouble. There is a corollary: The first thing you do when you *get* into trouble is, get *out* of trouble.

If you'll recite these companion rules every morning while you're talking to yourself in the shaving mirror, I can guarantee that you'll trim three strokes off your game.

Relax and Have a Blast!

The most common trouble shot in the game is the recovery from a sand trap. For the high-handicap player this also seems to be a fearful shot, a circumstance that is a little puzzling because it is one of the easiest shots on the course and, by far, the simplest trouble shot in the game. No other shot offers the player such a vast margin of safety.

Thirty minutes of concentrated practice should make any average golfer a confident—if not necessarily skilled—trap player. Yet, I doubt if there is one weekend golfer in a hundred who is ever willing to spend this minimum amount of practice time in a trap. And so he bumbles along, sailing and dribbling into bunkers and traps every weekend, and flailing away artlessly at a ball that stubbornly refuses to fly.

There are four basic types of sand shots. We'll take them in order of their complexity.

There is the ball that simply rolls into a firmly packed and very shallow trap. Now, if there is no lip on the green side of the trap, and you have nothing between you and the putting surface but smooth sand and a beard of fringe grass, don't be ashamed to run the ball out of there with a putter or a straight-faced iron. There are times when this is the safest shot to play. Just remember to hit the ball squarely and firmly. Guard against topping (usually the result of a hurried swing).

I don't recommend chipping out of sand. It can be done, but it's a delicate shot and should be reserved for the high roller.

Then there is the ball that rambles into soft sand for a clean lie. This is not an explosion shot, but the principle is the same. You have to swing the clubhead through the sand and beneath the ball, lifting it on a cushion of sand. We take our position comfortably at the ball, working our feet into the sand until we have a stable and well-balanced stance. At the same time, the positioning of our feet tells us something about the texture of the sand. Is it loose and fluffy? Then we can hit a good inch or more behind the ball, knowing the blade will slice through the grains easily. If it's a heavy sand, perhaps moist and tightly packed, we'll have to cut the blade in closer to the ball because we're going to encounter some resistance here.

This is a fine distinction you learn to make through practice and experience. It's not a matter of really great significance to you at an early stage of your golf education, but it will become increasingly important as your trap game improves and is refined.

The essential point to bear in mind with this shot is to relax, swing smoothly and easily—and swing *through* the shot. Don't quit on it. The sand wedge will play the shot all by itself if you give it half a chance. That's what it's designed for. The heavy flange on the sole of the club acts like an aileron on an airplane. Instead of boring deeper into the sand, it is inclined upward in a scooping arc which carries it under the ball and lifts it out of the sand in a soft, looping trajectory.

Of course, another important thing to remember at all times is the rule against grounding the club in the trap. This is an automatic penalty stroke. The ball must be addressed with a free-swinging blade and the backswing starts from a hovering position over the ball.

The sand shot is played with a lazy swing and a strong left hand. It's an abbreviated, three-quarter swing. We choke down on the shaft another inch and this, of course, reduces the arc of our swing accordingly. The club is carried back slowly and straightaway, and is brought back through the stroke firmly, but with no conscious or visible effort. Close the clubhead slightly and play the shot square against the target. The ball is played off the left toe.

It's important not to quit on the shot. Here is where the 90 shooter gets himself all fouled up. Governed by a morbid fear of the shot, he is either too timid or tries to overcompensate by muscling into the shot. In the first instance, he is usually playing slack-wristed and loses control of the club when it encounters the sand. In the second case, he hurries the swing, trying to overpower the shot, lunges at the ball and winds up throwing the clubhead into the sand—quitting cold on the shot. In either event, he fails to carry the clubhead through the shot.

If the ball is partially, or completely, buried in sand, you have an explosion shot. Again, there is a temptation to bore into the shot and this must be resisted. The shot is no more difficult than any other sand shot if you will continue to trust your swing and trust your club. Just remember, you have to make sure the blade passes beneath the ball, carrying it out on a cushion of sand. This means hitting a little farther behind the ball, perhaps 1½ to 2 inches.

The only trap shots that present any real problem are those where the ball comes to rest well forward in a steeply banked trap. Now you have a problem of getting the ball up quickly and over the rampart of the trap. This calls for the cut shot, a somewhat more delicate shot, but one that every golfer should carry in his bag. It is useful, too, in coming out of bad rough.

The cut shot, quite simply, is played like a deliberate and exaggerated slice. The idea is to bring the blade across and under the ball on a diagonal plane. This has the effect of laying the blade wide open so it can slice through the sand at a slightly deeper level, pushing sand forward and beneath the ball at the same time. In other words, as the ball is being excavated from its lie, this pressing wall of sand beneath and ahead of the ball acts to start it up on a steeper trajectory.

To play this shot we take an open stance, obliquely facing the target—usually the pin, although it could be that part of the green we have selected for our target. We bring the blade diagonally across the ball on an outside-in track, laying the blade open. Otherwise, the basic rules of sand play apply. Don't hurry the swing—and don't quit on the shot. Play it firmly and confidently.

A ball coming out of sand is going to run, although the cut shot will stop more quickly. Bear this in mind when you're surveying your escape route from the trap. If the pin is on the far side of a big green, you're in good shape. You have room to play. But if you're playing to a tight pin, placed on a narrow neck of green, discretion is the better part of valor. Play to the fat part of the green and hope for a good putt.

In fact, it's a pretty good general rule for the average high-handicap player to be satisfied just to get out of the trap and onto the putting surface.

The one trap shot that will really tie you up is the one you face when you have a buried ball directly under an overhanging crest of a deep bunker. There's not much anyone can do for you here but express sympathy. You're in real trouble and it's entirely possible that the best you can hope for is to shake the ball loose with the first blast and move it out to playing position.

And, by the way, don't overlook the possibility that you will one day face an impossible trap position and all you can do is play the ball laterally to a safe chipping position outside the trap.

Fairway traps offer a different set of conditions, permitting a full swing and the free use of the pitch shot (hitting the ball first, then taking sand). An important change in circumstance arises from the fact that we may be 100 to 175 yards from the green, clearly out of range of the sand irons and perhaps a full long-iron shot away.

Under these conditions, play the percentages. It's true that, in a shallow, firmly packed trap, there are times when a 4-wood can be used effectively. But don't yield to the temptation to attempt the impossible—or, at best, the unlikely. Very few long-iron shots out of traps ever reach the green. To attempt it, you may be digging yourself into even deeper trouble. Take a medium iron and play the shot you *know* will put the ball back in play—getting it down the fairway in position for an easy pitch or chip to the green.

Knowing when to take your losses is an important part of the strategy of the game and we'll discuss this at some length in a later chapter.

It's Rough, Man . . .

The second most common problem shot, and especially for the 90 shooter, is recovering from long grass—from the rough. The sand shot is an easy one. All it requires is enough practice to shake the phobia. But long grass is something else again. This is nothing to fool around with. It strangles more shots than any natural or artificial hazard on the course.

As in fairway traps, resist the temptation to try and escape your predicament and recover lost ground on the same shot. Never use a long iron out of this stuff. Calculate your chances. If you're satisfied you have a shot, draw the old 4-wood. Otherwise, go on down to your shorter-range irons—even to the wedge—and just play to get the ball back on the clover.

The only escape route from deep grass is by air. That means you want to get the ball up and flying as quickly as possible. So again, as in the steep-walled trap, we lay the face of the club open, open our stance and spin the ball out of there. Use a club with loft and weight, and hit down sharply with good wrist action. Don't sweep the club. The grass will tie you up, draining away all the force of the swing before the clubhead reaches the ball.

I remember finding myself in this predicament during one of the Shell television matches played in Copenhagen. I took two slashes at the ball to get out of the wiry rough, and I could be there yet if my first stroke hadn't shoved the ball onto a little wad of grass where I could get at it with my second.

Woodman, Spare That Shot

The third big shot-waster for the weekend golfer is the runaway ball that darts in among the trees. As I remarked earlier, the toughest part of this recovery shot is resisting the temptation to try the impossible. Leave those shots to one of the two immortal Walters—Hagen or Mitty.

There are only two escape routes out of the woods. You either go through an opening in the trees or come out under the branches. Think twice before you try to steer a ball through a narrow aperture. Consider the odds—and the consequences of failure.

Coming out from under trees is not a particularly difficult shot unless the branches are so low you can't swing a club. Then, of course, you *are* in trouble and the simplest way out is the only way out. And, if you find yourself in deep rough among the trees, your trouble is compounded and possibly the only thing you can do is to chip out to a better playing position.

Let's face it: there are situations in golf when you're dead. You have no shot. All you can do is move the ball far enough to change the conditions and get back in the game again.

But for the usual, uncomplicated recovery from among the trees, there are two requirements—a clear opening to the fairway or green, and a low-flying shot. The first requirement is a matter of personal judgment and, again, I can't emphasize too strongly that you allow plenty of margin for safety here. Don't gamble needlessly, and don't gamble foolishly.

A low shot is hit with a punch swing. This is one of the few occasions when I'll play the ball back of the center-line between my feet. For this one, we'll play it just inside the right foot, because we want the hands well ahead of the ball at the moment of impact, and we want to bring the face or blade of the club into the shot at a sharply reduced angle of loft.

We'll choke down an extra inch or so on the shaft of the club for tighter control of the shot. The club is taken back straight and low with a short, but unhurried backswing. Cock the wrists immediately as your right forearm reaches a horizontal position and bring the club back into the shot with the hands well in front all the way. Hit down and through, keeping the hands out ahead of the ball even after it's hit.

Conversely, there will be occasions when you will want to get the ball up quickly, into a higher trajectory. It goes without saying that the procedure is reversed. The ball is played well forward toward the left toe, and a conscious effort is made to let the clubhead pass the hands and move into the ball on a sharply inclined plane.

This is not an easy shot, by any means. It's a flip shot, with lots of wrist action. It requires split-second timing of the swing and an extremely accurate gauging of the point of impact. What we're doing on this shot, of course, is violating the very basic rule that applies to virtually every other shot. We're "scooping" the ball, but doing it expertly. This is not a shot for the 100 shooter.

Hillside Lies

Hillside lies are not exactly trouble shots in the true sense of the word because, on many courses, you can encounter this type of lie in some degree with most shots. Nevertheless, they do present a special difficulty requiring you to alter the basic pattern of your stance or your swing and, consequently, we'll deal with them here.

There are four general types of hillside lies: the downhill lie, the uphill lie and the sidehill lies—both up and down. Then, of course, there are combination lies on slopes that fall away or rise both laterally and lineally. These are just exercises in adjustment, bringing to bear what you know about playing the two types of slopes that are combining.

The downhill lie is one where the ground slopes away from you toward the hole. (You are standing with the right foot higher than the left.) There are two important things to remember here: (1) There is a natural tendency to slice the shot, and (2) a temptation to scoop, or pick up, the ball. Go to a shorter club than you would normally select for the distance. Bear in mind, a 7-iron is going to play like a 5-iron because the natural slope of the terrain cancels out much of the loft of the club.

This is an apparent contradiction. With the ground sloping away in front of you, you would expect that the angle of inclination on the face of the club would be accented— changing a 5-iron to a 7-iron. The opposite is true. The reason: the slope is short-stopping your swing, bringing the club into the ball before it reaches what should be the bottom of your swing arc.

For this shot, let's play the ball back a little toward the right foot and close the club-face just a little. This is to safeguard against the natural slice and to help keep the shot going out straight. Shorten the grip and take a trial swing to establish your arc. Flex your uphill knee to keep your hips on a level plane.

Hit down and through the shot and resist the temptation to help the ball on its way. Leave the whole job to the club and don't be suckered into using a longer club than you should. Remember: *The downhill lie cancels out some of the club's built-in loft.*

The uphill lie offers another apparent contradiction. You would expect to go to a club with more loft to get the ball up in the air quickly against a rising slope. Instead, we use a more straight-faced club and don't try to hit down on the ball quite as much as we would playing a flat lie. Play the ball forward of the center-line, about off the left heel, because it's going to be a little difficult to go through the shot. Gravity is always pulling us backward and off balance, and to maintain our balance we should shade our weight over to the left leg and sort of "lean" into the shot, but not noticeably. Again, the idea is to keep the hips level.

All these adjustments for hillside lies are only adjustments of slight degree. Don't exaggerate them. Balance is the key to carrying off these shots successfully, and all your stance and swing adjustments are made solely to maintain a balanced position at the ball. With good balance, there is no problem in staying down with the shot to a full finish, and you have to stay with these shots all the way or you'll mess them up.

On all uphill lies there is a strong tendency to pull, or hook, the ball. Open the face of the club a little and aim to the right of the target. On downhill lies, the situation is reversed. To overcome a tendency to push, or slice, we close the face of the club somewhat and aim for a point to the left of the pin.

The downhill-sidehill lie (when you are standing above the ball) offers a strong attraction for the slice. Close the face of the club a little and aim to the left of the target. Because the ball is lying below its usual position in relation to the hands, we should stand a little closer to the ball and grip the club at its limit. The knees should be flexed just a little more than usual, emphasizing the "sitting" position. Most important thing of all on this shot, however, is not to vary the rhythm of your swing and stay down with the shot all the way through to a high finish.

The uphill-sidehill lie (when you're standing below the ball) figures to play just the opposite, of course. Weight should be forward on the balls of the feet, and we choke up a little more on the shaft because we want to compensate for the shorter swing arc. Allowance must be made for the tendency to draw, or hook, this shot. We open the face slightly and aim for a point to the right of the pin. The swing should be flatter than usual.

Balance, as I said, is awfully important in playing all hillside shots. Gravity is always dragging us away from, or pushing us into, the shot. This gravitational pull may not be too noticeable when we're addressing the ball, but it's

attraction is multiplied when we swing because it is rein-
forced by the force of the swing. But all our adjustments are
subtle ones because the gravitational influence we are trying
to neutralize is subtle.

Water—and Other Problems

The best advice I can offer for playing a ball out of
water is—don't. Rarely will you have even a fighting chance
of recovering from this hazard with any degree of effectiveness. Of course, 99 times out of 100 you won't even be able
to retrieve the ball.

However, there are occasions when the ball rolls into
the shallow margin of a water hazard, offering a possible
chance to recover. Possibly, the hazard is close to the green
and you see a glimmering hope of coming out in putting
position.

I would say that, if any part of the ball is protruding
above the surface of the water, you can have a go at it as a
sporting gesture. A ball in water is played very much like a
ball buried in sand, or lying in thick rough. It's an explosion shot. Use a wedge or a 9-iron and play a cut shot. Only
the cut shot, with the blade slicing through the water at an
oblique angle, can possibly carry through the solid resistance
of water, squirting the ball out of there and riding on
through to a finish.

But before you tackle this shot, consider the odds.
Unless you're within a few yards of the green, you'd do well
to play the percentage. Drop out and take your penalty
because, even if you succeed in spraying your way out of the
water, you aren't going any place with the shot and the few
yards you'll gain on the shot can easily be recovered with
an honest shot from a decent lie.

Among the other problem shots are these:

Digging a ball out of a divot hole. This is a punch shot.
Play the ball back of the center-line with the weight shaded
to the left, then hit down on the ball with your hands ahead
of the ball.

Playing a ball lying close to a fence. If the fence is facing you as you address the ball, close the face of the club so the ball will hook back to safety, and swing easily. If the fence prevents you from taking your position at the ball, you will have to play a left-handed shot. This is done by reversing your hand positions and rolling the club over so the toe becomes the sole. Be sure and use a broad-faced club for this shot and don't expect much more from the shot than to get the ball back in play. Furthermore, it's a shot that takes practice before attempting it.

Playing a ball off bare ground. Again we have the punch-type shot. Get the hands out there ahead of the club and hit the ball before hitting the ground. Otherwise, your club may bounce and you'll top the shot.

There will be any number of instances where you'll be faced with a restricted swing—beneath trees, against obstructions of one kind and another. There's a great danger of lunging at this shot, hoping to make up with brute force the distance you know you're going to have to sacrifice. Don't attempt this. Measure your backswing carefully so you get your maximum swing arc, and then hit through firmly and smoothly. Don't hurry the swing and don't panic.

6

How to practice

"Work and Win"

'Way back when the century was young and the world was square, there was a square writer of boys' books, with the square name of Horatio Alger, who had some square ideas that were reflected in the titles of his books. They ran to alliteration, like *Strive and Succeed,* and *Work and Win.*

This was before the grifter and the hustler wormed his way into our lives, and the angle-shooter began shooting holes in the fabric of our society. Today, about 50 per cent of the population are firmly sold on the proposition that only horses work. The other 50 per cent would be inclined to go along with this sentiment except that they never saw a horse.

I'm not out to reform the world, but I do cling to a few tattered old virtues—like believing you don't get anything for nothing in this world. And I've lived long enough to be convinced that this is one of those eternal verities that will be around long after I've sunk my last putt and gone to that great 19th hole in the sky.

I didn't learn to play golf on a golf course, strange as it may sound. Nor, for that matter, did any other man I know who plays golf for a living. We learned our art, and developed it to a high degree of perfection, on the practice range. That's where I played the shots that won me the British Open championship in 1964. That's where I hit the draw shot that birdied three holes for me in the Buick Open that same year.

Every golf professional you see out on the P.G.A. tour is the product of thousands of hours of practice. Every shot that he can anticipate on the course is played over and over and over on the practice tee until it can be performed almost automatically, the way a pianist plays a Chopin sonata that he has slaved over at the keyboard.

Practicing is a lonely and often discouraging exercise, whether you're working your way through a set of matched irons or Tschaikowsky's "Polonaise." But there is no easy way, or gregarious way, to acquire mastery of an art. You have to work at it.

Ben Hogan was a product of the practice tee. Conceivably, Hogan is the greatest golfer the world has ever seen. Yet, he had to put his flawless game together by painful stages, shot by shot. I doubt if there ever has been a golfer who has been such a slave to the practice tee. He set a standard of devotion to practice that had a whole generation of golf pros wearing out practice tees. Oldtimers shook their heads in dismay and insisted the pros were leaving a lot of their best shots on the practice range. But it was a method that suited Hogan, and his competitive record testifies to its effectiveness.

I don't recommend that the average golfer, who plays for sport and light exercise, burn the midnight oil on the practice tee the way Hogan did. In fact, on the contrary, I recommend practice in light doses for the fun-golfer. It isn't the *hours* you put in at practice that count. It's the way you spend those *minutes*. There's no point in knocking out yourself on the practice tee to no purpose, then drag yourself over to the starting tee for a grinding trip around the course. That kind of practice is self-defeating.

Practice should be constructive. It should be refreshing, because from it you should derive a fresh shot of confidence in your game. You should learn something from it—but one thing at a time is enough. You build a golf game like you build a wall, one brick at a time.

Warming Up

I don't believe in practicing or starting out on a round without warming up. The man who rushes from his office to the golf club, gulps a sandwich, belches and races to the first tee has no business howling in anguish when he puts his first two shots in the woods, then tops a 3-iron shot into the pond. Yet, this is the same guy who never hit a 3-iron off the practice tee in his life—and wonders why his card is always sprinkled with 7s and 8s.

Because warming up is closely related to practice, we'll discuss both aspects of the game in this chapter.

Before I hit a single golf ball, I go to work loosening up my muscles. Some of these muscles have been doing something else—perhaps driving the car, or lifting and carrying things. I figure I have to get their attention and remind them we're about to do something else. Other muscles have been quietly snoozing, waiting for the call to duty. These muscles have to be waked up and put to work. They all have to start functioning smoothly and rhythmically together, fusing into a cohesive flow of physical force.

So, I borrow a little exercise from the baseball batter. I'll take two clubs in a baseball grip and just swing them freely for a couple of minutes, gradually widening the arc of my swing until I can feel a looseness and suppleness in the shoulders and through the large muscles of the back.

Meanwhile, my hips are shifting laterally and swivelling on a horizontal plane until I sense my whole body is moving easily like a ball-bearing in a socket. Even the muscles in my feet are reacting to the rocking transfer of my weight. They are being conditioned, too, for their important role in maintaining a solid and balanced stance.

When I feel my muscles are toned up and ready to respond to the demands of the golf swing, I start to warm up. Now, some professionals methodically go down the line, starting at either end of the club set, and hitting balls with every club until they are satisfied. Personally, I'm inclined to believe this is over-doing the warm-up bit. You could be leaving a lot of good shots on the practice tee.

Instead, I like to start with the 9-iron, let's say, and work my way down through the range of irons in a leap-frog pattern, hitting four or five shots with all the odd-numbered clubs—the 7-, the 5- and the 3-. By then I've steadily widened the arc of my swing and I'm ready to wrap up the session with a few good cracks with the 4-wood and the driver.

The next time out, I may start with the wedge and progress down through the even-numbered irons, winding up always with the same two woods.

I don't worry about how I'm hitting the ball when I'm warming up. All I'm interested in is getting my muscles into play and sharpening the timing of my swing. Oh, with each club I'll try bending the ball on the last two or three shots. I'll hit a draw, and then a fade. But I'm not looking for perfection here. I'm just interested in getting the feel of each club and sort of jogging my shot-making memory.

And now that I'm warmed up, I'm ready to move along to the practice green on my way to the first tee—or, I'm ready to begin some serious practice.

Practice with a Purpose

The most common practice error is to drift aimlessly out to the practice tee and start banging balls at random. This isn't practice. This is just a waste of time and you'd be better off out on the course. At least, out there you'd be firing at live targets.

The worst thing you can do is go out and practice your errors.

You should never approach the practice range without a purpose, without a problem to be solved. And, it should follow from this that, when that particular problem has been solved, or at least reduced to tolerable proportions, the practice session is over. Never hang around the practice tee looking for new trouble.

Ideally, each practice session should be devoted exclusively to the main source of aggravation during your last playing round.

You were smothering your fairway wood shots? Okay, then book an appointment with your club pro, if you belong to a club, and work it out with him. If you play free-lance, public links golf and prefer to struggle with your own problems, seek some advice. Read a book. Find out the probable cause of your trouble. Failing that, just take your fairway woods to the practice tee and work exclusively on them. Check your grip, your stance, your swing. Work slowly and thoughtfully, starting at the beginning and rebuilding the swing. Build to confidence and, when you have recovered your confidence in these shots, bang them out there joyfully until you're satisfied you've got the monkey off your back.

Then stop.

As I remarked earlier, unless you learn something from your practice session, you've wasted your time. By now, you should have a pretty clear idea of (1) why you were smothering these shots the last time out, or (2) at least what you did to get the ball flying again. You won't always discover (1) without professional guidance, but you certainly should come away with a clue to (2).

If you have no specific and immediate problem, you always have a general problem. There are certain clubs in the bag which you seldom use. Why? Probably because you don't hit them well and lack confidence in them.

I know a man who will play a soft 5-iron or lean into a 7-iron before he will draw the 6-iron for a 6-iron shot. It's an idiosyncracy, without any rational basis. It's a case, pure and simple, of a golfer developing an early confidence in and affection for two clubs at the expense of the in-between club.

When I questioned him about it, it developed that, as a kid, he had a broken set of irons which included only the

Nos. 3, 5 and 7. He played with these clubs for years and acquired a confidence in them. Like the old golfer of the nineteenth century, he learned to play all shots with a limited set of tools. When, eventually, he could afford to own a full set, he continued to play his familiar game. The 6-iron never came out of the bag. Nor would he ever take the time to go to the practice tee and hit with that 6-iron until it became a trusted old friend.

A very common weakness among the high-handicap players is an inability to hit a long iron with authority. As we observed in Chapter 2, the 2-iron and 3-iron give the once-in-a-while golfer a lot of trouble because the hitting surface is relatively small. And the shafts are longer, requiring a wider arc to the swing with a greater margin for error.

The shank, the slice and hook, the fat shot and the topped shot—these are all common faults when the weekend golfer draws a long iron from the bag.

So, if you have no immediate and absorbing problem, but suffer from chronic long-iron fatigue, here's your ticket to the practice tee. Instead of going out there and whacking away absentmindedly with those clubs you already hit well and consistently, limit yourself to the 2- and 3-iron, and just work with them for thirty minutes. If you go out there just to hit your favorite shot and watch it fly in silent admiration, forget it!

And I mentioned a period of time—thirty minutes. That's long enough. I know Ben Hogan used to spend an hour or two at practice. But you aren't Hogan, and neither is anybody else. I don't care who you are, after thirty minutes of sustained concentration, your practice efforts can't go anywhere but downhill. It's like a party after 2 A.M. If you're still looking for the party at that time, you'll never find it. She's gone home.

Have a Target

Except when you're warming up (and then only to a degree), never hit a golf ball without a target in mind. It may be the pin on a distant green. It may be only an imaginary spot on the fairway. But always have some place in mind where you expect the ball to come to rest. Otherwise, you're just launching rockets into space for the pleasure of watching the glow from the after-burners.

Even on the practice tee every shot should be aimed— somewhere. If you're working on your woods, for instance, it isn't enough just to put the ball into a gratifying trajectory. While you're at it, you might as well have a down-range target. It doesn't cost you any more. Play to one side or the other of the hypothetical fairway. Select a swale or a slope, or some other physical feature on the range, and try to lay the ball out there somewhere in relation to it.

Here, on the practice tee, is where you learn to play the draw shot and the fade. Each type of shot should be a self-contained lesson. In fact, you probably won't learn to hit either type of shot in one thirty-minute practice session. These are the refinements, the nuances, of the art. They will require time to master. But, bear in mind, it is here, on the practice tee, they will be learned—not by hitting an occasional experimental shot out there on the golf course.

Finally, get professional guidance—at least periodically or when you have a special problem that doesn't resolve itself in lonely practice.

The Practice Green

Probably no part of the game of golf gets more practice —and, at the same time, less practice—than putting. This apparent contradiction can be explained readily. The average golfer, the fellow who joins his foursome every Saturday morning or Sunday afternoon, rarely visits the practice tee. But you'll find him on the practice putting green every week—if for no other reason than to kill time until the rest of the foursome arrive, or until the starter calls him to the first tee.

In other words, he puts in a lot of time on the practice green, but never really practices. He just fiddles around, warms up and gets the feel of hitting the ball at the pin. And putting being the rite that it is, fiddling may be enough unless he has a serious problem.

Actually, you don't *practice* putting in the sense that you practice playing the 7-iron or the trap shot. Putting is a mystique, compounded of three parts confidence and one part style. You have to believe firmly, in your heart, that the ball can go no place else but in the cup. Then you just hit it.

And so, this is one golf shot where practice plays only a small part. You could practice all day long, then have a ten-year-old kid come along and putt the pants off you simply because he doesn't know enough to be afraid of a putt.

Furthermore, since every green has its own individuality, and I've never encountered two identical putts in my life, practice is only an accumulation of experience. And here's a case where experience is the best teacher—but only up to a point. Beyond that, all you're doing is batting a ball around a smooth lawn.

We have discussed putting at length in a separate chapter and there's no point in reviewing that material here. But we are concerned here with practice methods and a word or two on the subject of sharpening the putting touch is appropriate.

Four things can happen to a putt. It can go wide of the hole on either side. It can run beyond the hole. It can die short of the hole. And it can go *in* the hole. The successful putt, the one that runs into the hole, is a happy combination of line and distance.

This is an over-simplification, of course. But putting is, basically, a simple exercise. It becomes complicated when the nervous system becomes involved. Now, there isn't much you can do about the nervous system on the practice green. But you can take some practical steps toward controlling the physical factors involved—the line and distance of the putt.

In the final analysis, all putting practice is aimed at one thing: reducing or eliminating the three-putt factor in our game. The pro, of course, expects to get around eighteen holes in not more than 32 putts. The standard card allocates two putts per hole, but he figures to one-putt at least four greens if he hopes to make a comfortable living at this game. You can imagine how devastating a three-putt green is to him!

For the high-handicap player, the stakes aren't as high and, if he can take his regulation thirty-six putts, he'll play up to his potential. But even he can't afford to throw away strokes on the green. To him, the three-putt green is a goblin that is always standing there, grinning at him, when he reaches for his putter because his first putt is invariably a long one.

I've spent some time here building a case, because I have a point to make and it governs the approach to practice putting.

When I go to the practice green, I always start putting from a distance of about 8 feet because this is the putt the pro has to make for his birdie. When I throw the ball up to the pin, I usually find it somewhere in this radius from the cup.

Now, from a distance of 8 to 10 feet, the pro has a problem with a two-way stretch. He wants to run that putt down. So he has to hit the ball so it will run just far enough to reach the cup—and along a line that will carry it to that point.

What about the 90 shooter? When he reaches the green, he may be anywhere from 10 to 30 feet from the hole. If he runs his first putt in, he has combined a measure of skill with an awful lot of luck. But if he misses his *second* putt, he's just a poor putter who didn't learn his lesson on the practice green.

This has been a roundabout way to get to the point, but the point I want to make is important if you're a typical 90 shooter (and the playing statistics tell me I have a 1-to-10 shot going for me here). When you reach the green your immediate problem, nine times out of ten, is to lay the ball up there close enough to the hole for a copper-riveted cinch on your second putt. Remember, those long lag putts rarely stray more than 4 or 5 *inches* off line. But you set yourself up for a third putt when the ball dies *yards* short of the cup —or gallops several feet beyond.

This is why I strongly recommend that high-handicap players concentrate on what you might call "putting depth perception," getting the feel of rolling the ball up there for an easy second putt. Sharpen your touch with these long putts, then move into birdie country for real target practice from 10 feet and closer.

In summary, always practice with a purpose. Aimless practicing is a waste of time. Have a problem to resolve, or a specific objective to achieve. Concentrate on it, and on what you're doing. When you've mastered your problem or accomplished your immediate objective, put the clubs back in the bag. School's out for the day.

Finally, if possible, seek out a professional and work with him. It will save you a lot of time and spare you a lot of frustration.

7

Playing percentage golf

The Thinking Man's Game

The par-3 16th hole at Cypress Point, where Bing Crosby stages his annual "clambake," is a real booby trap. The green sticks up there on a promontory against the Pacific Ocean. The card says it's 220 yards from the tee, but it usually plays more like 240 to 250 yards.

Now, if you're going to play golf by the book, you've got to fire out for the green. And, as sure as you do, you're a brass-bound cinch to wind up shopping for scuba gear. Very few pros go for the green on this hole. Usually, we lay the ball up there on the fore side and gamble on a chip and a putt for our par. Even a bogey here is better than carrying down to the rocks and trying to recover. Porky Oliver holds the record for this one—nineteen strokes! He found the Pacific Ocean is a lot bigger than the green.

The 16th at Cypress Point is an object lesson in not letting the golf architect bamboozle you.

A golf course is a piece of real estate that has been artfully rearranged by a landscape artist who specializes in
thinking up diabolical schemes to frustrate a golfer. No, let's
amend that statement. Actually, the architect is interested
only in punishing stupidity and bumbling, and rewarding
fine strokes. But, being human, he sometimes can't resist
the temptation to sucker you into disaster.

That 16th hole at Cypress Point is an example. Wit-
tingly or unwittingly, aided and abetted by the treacherous
winds that dance in off the Pacific, the architect has set up
a situation where only the boldest shot, played with consum-
mate skill, earns a reward. However, the risks are so great
and the reward so modest that most of us pros refuse flatly
to take the bait. Instead of playing the hole as a par 3, we
play it, so to speak, as a par-4 birdie hole.

I cite this example because, if you hope to score well in
this game, you have to learn to play what is called "percentage golf." That is, you have to learn to size up a situation
quickly and decide on a course of action. You have to consider always the factor of the little man who isn't there
(but *has* been there!)—the architect. It isn't always enough
to hammer a ball along the fairway toward a distant green.
You have to have at least a general plan for attacking the hole.
You have to select what, in your judgement, is the best or
the safest route from tee to green. And, as special situations
arise along the way, you must be able to analyze them,
calculate the odds and make your play with intelligence and
confidence.

For instance, let's set up a hypothetical par-4 hole with
a sharp dogleg to the right about 200 yards out there. At
the point of the dogleg there is a heavy stand of trees and
undergrowth and, from the turn of the dogleg, the fairway
slopes away toward the green. I'm sure you've played this
hole, or one very much like it, somewhere along the line.
I've played it a hundred times, all over the country.

Obviously, if you can bend your tee shot around the
corner, or shave the corner, you'll catch the downslope for a
nice little extra run of the ball, leaving you a comfortable

mid-iron shot to the green. It's a tempting prospect, and the fact that you've carried it off a couple of times makes the temptation doubly hard to resist.

But let's weigh the odds.

If you fail to turn the corner, if your fade drifts off into the trees, your second shot is a tough one at best—and perhaps you'll have no shot at all. If you elect to flush the ball out of the woods, you're working your way to one of those 7s or 8s that always wreck your round.

What if you choose the alternate route: lay the ball out there straightaway from the tee, then play a second wood at right angles, sticking to the middle of the fairway? You have just as good a chance to lay the ball up there with a 4-wood as you have with a 4-iron. This is the sensible way to play the hole. The dogleg is a booby trap. The architect is tempting you with the rosy prospect of—what? Just a chance to get within comfortable iron range of the green. But when you weigh this meager reward against the horror that lurks in wait if your tee shot strays, clearly the percentages are all in favor of laying down two safe woods at right angles.

Now, let's revise the conditions. Let's imagine this same hole is stretched out to a par 5, to a point where a well-played tee shot that bends around the corner and catches the slope can set you up for a long carry to the green and a possible birdie. Now we have a completely different equation. The reward, in the form of a birdie, justifies the risk, assuming that your skills are up to tackling the shot.

This is playing percentage golf.

It calls to mind the Buick Open in 1962. The second hole at Warwick Hills in Flint is one of these par-5 doglegs to the right. You can't make the turn with your tee shot, but it's possible, by cutting the corner with your second, to put the ball up there in front of the green for a shot at a birdie. In the final round I was in perfect position for this tactical maneuver and I hit what I thought was a fine 5-iron shot that should have arched over the trees and dropped into ideal position.

I don't know what that ball hit, but it was something mighty solid. I wound up out of bounds, clear across the fairway and almost out of the money. But the situation called for the gamble. It might have paid off handsomely. It was percentage golf.

I'm reminded of the story they tell of Ben Hogan and Sam Snead when these two great players were teamed on the American side in the Canada Cup matches at Wentworth, England. The two played a practice round together. For Hogan, probably the game's finest strategist, it was his first look at the course where, a couple of days later, he would set a new course record. Snead, on the other hand, had played that course a couple of years before, and lost his singles match in the Ryder Cup event.

After they finished their round, Ben sat down with Sam and said, "Sam, you're not playing this course right. To begin with, you should leave your driver in the bag. It won't do you any good here. Use a 4-wood or an iron off the tee...."

Then he went on, hole by hole, to analyze the course and counsel Snead on how to attack it successfully.

When he came to the 17th hole, where Sam had lost his Ryder Cup match to Harry Weetman, Hogan said, "You know how the fairway goes out about 200 yards, then slopes away? Don't put your tee shot over the crest of that slope because you can't get a good lie on the other side...."

This ability to explore a golf course and develop all its latent dangers made Ben Hogan the greatest golfer of his generation, and perhaps of all time. He never attacked a hole blindly. He never hit a "Hail Mary" shot. He never repeated a mistake and, as he reached his peak, rarely made one. Hogan was not above gambling when the circumstances called for it. But with Hogan the element of risk was reduced to zero because he always knew the course and he knew his own game. The rest was just execution of the shot—and Ben always played the right shot.

In that same conversation, he dissected another hole at Wentworth and his analysis deserves to be filed away in some cerebral pigeon hole because it can be applied universally to all similar holes. He cited one hole in particular where the green sloped upward from the approach.

"Play this hole short all the way," he told Snead. "Come into the green short because the pin has to be back there somewhere and you'll want to be putting up to it." Given his druthers, any sane golfer will prefer to putt uphill rather than try to cozy the ball downhill to the cup.

Always remember, there's a time to play safe and a time to gamble. Let's consider another hypothetical situation. Let's imagine a par-5 hole with the pin set at the back of the green and a water hazard lying about 10 to 15 yards in front of the green. For the fun of it, let's picture the 15th at the Augusta National, with the creek winding across the front of the green.

With a helluva good wood from the fairway, after a booming drive, you might clear the creek for a go at birdying the hole. But there's no percentage here in gambling for the bird, not when you have to stretch your best wood shot to carry over that water. And don't remind me that Gene Sarazen scored his double eagle here in 1935! When you can win both the U.S. and British Open championships, you can play any kind of a damfool shot you like.

I might add, incidentally, that Gene had everything to win and not much to lose when he went for bust on that one. Percentage golf!

Beware of any situation that calls for you to hit the shot of your career to bail you out. If you're an 80 to 90 player, you're going to run into a lot of golfers who play your game. Shot for shot, there won't be much to choose between you. So, it's the best thinker, the one with the best mental attitude, who wins.

It's a good general tactical rule to play the ball to the "fat" part of the course: down the middle of the fairway and to the center of the green. If you can keep the ball in play and keep it rolling at the hole, consistency of this kind has a way of adding its own bonuses to the regular rewards.

The standard green has an opening between a couple of traps or hazards. Normally, your safest approach to the pin is through this gate, and you will try to place your ball in a position to make this approach. This is what we call "opening up" the green.

Rarely is this gate facing you directly as you approach along the fairway. Usually, the direct approach is barred by a yawning trap that cuts deeply into the fairway, and the opening is on one side or the other. This means, of course, that your best approach to the green is along that side of the fairway which will present you with a fair shot to the green through the opening. This becomes your strategic plan for attacking the hole.

In all probability, however, the golf course architect will have anticipated you by trapping the route, or taking advantage of the natural terrain to impede your progress. For instance, perhaps the fairway slopes away to the right and a ball played to that side of the fairway stands a good chance of being carried off into the rough.

Now, instead of a simple and uncomplicated decision, you are faced with a full-blown dilemma involving two critical factors. You want to move the ball along the right side of the fairway, but the terrain makes this a very risky tightrope-walking exercise. What to do?

Well, first you take another hard look at the green. Is it a large green and, from your knowledge of it, will it hold a well-hit shot? Is the pin placed well back? Often as not, you'll be hitting to an elevated plateau green and all you'll be able to see is the flag and the top of the stick. You'll have to guesstimate where the cup has been cut. But you look for these answers because the usual safe approach to the green is fraught with peril, and it's time to reconsider the possibility of playing to the high side of the fairway and coming into the green with a lofted shot over the guardian trap.

One of the toughest holes I have ever encountered is a par 5 at Fuji, in Japan. This one has a regular camelback running down the center of the fairway and your ball kicks off to one side or the other. With a little luck, you'll hold to the rim of the fairway with a shot at a green that is guarded by two immense sand craters, back to back. This is one I'd enjoy watching Hogan play. I didn't fathom it.

Earlier in this book, when we were discussing the various clubs, I said I regarded the drive the most important shot in the bag. I say this for two reasons. First, you have to put the ball out there with the other boys if you expect to stay with them. Second, the tee shot is the one that puts you in position to attack the hole. Which leads me to an apparent contradiction when I say the second shot on most holes is the payoff shot.

This is the shot we're setting ourselves up for when we drive. On any regulation golf course, the majority of the holes are par 4s, meaning you should be able to reach the green with your second shot. It follows, then, that all your strategy should be directed toward giving yourself every possible advantage for this shot. Even on the par-5 holes this second shot has a special meaning. It's the birdie-maker.

The Augusta National course, where the Masters championship is played each spring, is designed with one thing in mind: to reward the bold and successful second shot. As Bobby Jones, its creator, described it to me: "Augusta is not a difficult course for the weekend amateur who is frankly looking for bogeys. But for the player who is out for pars and birdies, it can be a real tough course."

The same can be said for Pinehurst No. 2, another great golf course. The bogey-hunter can roam without fear. But the par shooter has to know exactly what he's doing—and do it—or he'll be punished.

Whereas the tee shot is a bomber and a straight power play, the second shot calls for accuracy of line and judgment of distance. Let's go back and take another look at that situation we discussed a few moments ago. We'll assume we've abandoned the approach along the right side of the fairway as being too perilous to be practical. So we're left with two alternatives as we stand up to our second shot: whether to bang away at the green and try to carry that trap, or play short of the trap for a pitch and a putt.

Naturally, if we're gunning for par, the decision already is made for us. We'll fire out for the green. But let's assume we're a 90 shooter with dreams of getting into the low 80s. Our chances of carrying that trap are no better than 50-50 —with only a 50-50 hope of stopping the ball on the green if we do.

Now our decision can depend largely on how well we're hitting the ball, on our confidence. If we're playing poorly, discretion is always the better part of valor. We play to conserve strokes—a conservative game, literally. When we're hitting the ball well and our confidence is building with every stroke, that's the time to play boldly—boldly but not foolishly. Always gear your game to your mental attitude. Bear in mind, the game is largely an exercise in mental discipline. If you learn to play within your capabilities, you'll find that extra reserve of surprising skill when you need it.

The top-handicap holes on the card always figure to be long and bristling with trouble. That's why they're rated for handicap allowance. Play these holes warily. Be humble. Go out of your way to sidestep trouble on these holes because there's a sleeping demon somewhere along the route and you don't want to disturb him.

It only makes good sense to play our best shots from a good clean fairway lie, not out of a trap 191 yards from the green. That's why it also makes sense to stay out of those traps, even if it means plotting a course well away from some pitfall, or throttling down your swing to lay the ball up safely short of trouble. I don't regard this as "steering" the ball. I call it simply conserving your strength and your golf game by keeping the ball in playing position at all times.

The temptation to buck the odds usually overcomes you as a result of a misplayed shot. Here is where most errors of judgment originate on a golf course. A poor shot puts you at a disadvantage and you throw caution to the winds in a wild and unreasoning attempt to retrieve your position.

We discussed this subject in the chapter on trouble shots. It's worth reviewing here because it involves a tactical approach to the game. It involves decision-making of the highest order, and golf, to a large extent, is a game in which the prize goes to the level-headed player who gives ground grudgingly in the face of disaster and refuses to be stampeded into total disorder, or to be borne along on a wave of panic.

Faulty judgment, by the way, isn't a weakness that is limited to the high-handicap amateur. Every professional on the tour has bitter memories of instances when he let his imagination run away with his common sense—and paid for it with a hole score that erased his entire tournament effort. Let me tell you a story.

Back in 1963 I was playing at Palm Springs, on the final hole of a ninety-hole tournament. As I stepped up on the 90th tee I looked like a solid bet to finish among the top five, which meant a good week's pay for a journeyman golf professional. Even after I topped my second shot badly, I still could bogey the hole and wind up sixth. But instead of taking an iron and running the ball up close enough for an easy pitch to the green with a faint hope of salvaging my par, I elected to try a wood and go for the green in a desperate bid to recover my lost shot. This was my first mistake: trying to dig the ball out of a bad fairway lie with a wood. The ball failed to reach the green and, perversely, dribbled down the embankment of one of two water traps that guarded the green.

The ball was stopped from trickling into the water by the long grass bordering the pond. Now I was faced with an impossible shot out of this sedge at the edge of the pond, across some 18 feet of water that lay between me and the green. I could have dropped back at the cost of a penalty stroke (and about $400 or $500 in prize money), and chipped onto the green for a 7. But I still wasn't smart enough to take the penalty and get out of a bad situation as gracefully as I could. No, I had to be stubborn about it—my second mistake.

I took my sand iron and laid the blade wide open after taking off my shoes and socks and taking a stance, half in and half out of the water. I swung, and the blade went cleanly under the ball, which jumped up and then settled back into the divot hole again. There was a pretty good gallery there who found the performance good for a laugh.

Well, I still refused to accept the blunt fact that I was dealing with an impossible shot, so I made my third mistake in the series. I tried again. This time I got the ball up and flying, but not far enough to reach the green. It landed on the far slope and slid back down the embankment into the water. Around on the green side of the pond I threw away some more strokes, including a couple of penalty strokes when I inadvertently "grounded" my club in the water hazard. Then I lofted the ball over the green into the twin water hazard on the other side.

It all added up to a memorable thirteen strokes and I paid dearly for my stupidity by finishing one stroke out of the money. My one mistake, compounded by a whole chain of consequent errors, wiped out all that I had worked for that week. Instead of coming away from Palm Springs with a good week's pay, I came away with empty pockets and a harsh lesson in playing percentage golf.

The Power of Positive Thinking

Golf, as a sporting pastime, is unique, I believe. It involves neither the bodily contact of many team sports, nor the explosive release of muscular energy required in various forms of competition. While it does involve the actual physical act of striking a ball, the golf stroke itself is only the end result of a period of preparation that hinges on intense mental concentration and nerve control. It's a game that is about 70 per cent mental, and 30 per cent physical. Self-discipline is the key to success.

If I had to cram all my tournament experience into one capsule of counsel, I would say, "Don't give up and don't let up!" You can be the most lovable guy in the grille, but out there on the course you've got to develop a heart of stone. When you've got your opponent two down, don't rest until you've got him three down. And when he's three down, you've got to figure he's three times as dangerous. Get him four down.

Al Watrous once had Bobby Cruickshank eleven down with thirteen holes to play in the thirty-six-hole P.G.A. championship, back when that tournament was conducted at match play. In a magnanimous mood, he conceded Bobby a 5-foot putt for a half at the 24th hole. When Cruickshank saw the door opening like that, he bolted through and won eleven of the next twelve holes to square the match. Then he went on to win it at the seventh extra hole!

By the same token, Cruickshank's performance should serve as an object lesson in refusing to accept defeat.

I don't know whether Norman Vincent Peale was ever much of a golfer, but the clergyman who coined the phrase, "The Power of Positive Thinking," qualified as the golfer's chaplain. If I had to choose between an optimist and a pessimist for a golfing partner, I wouldn't hesitate to pick the optimist. And not because of his sunny disposition, necessarily, nor his club handicap. Rather, because I know from experience that the guy who believes in happy endings is going to play consistently better golf than the man who approaches every act of existence with fear and foreboding.

When you stand up to a shot, you have to have a vivid mental picture of yourself executing the shot successfully. If you're faced with a delicate pitch shot over a trap to the green, your chances of carrying it off are excellent if you have the capacity for running off a quick little mental motion picture of yourself playing the shot. On the other hand, if all you can see is the ball squirting into the trap, you're 9-to-1 to put it there.

This buoyant, positive approach to the game is as basic, I believe, as a sound swing. Of course, a good swing and mastery of the necessary shots breeds a natural confidence that is reflected in a positive attitude. The "Compleat Golfer" is such an intricate thing, such a tightly woven fabric of mental and physical discipline, that each part contributes to the functioning of another and, in turn, borrows from still another part. The whole thing becomes a finely integrated machine, part bone and sinew and part brain impulses. As long as discipline sits at the controls, this delicately balanced machine operates smoothly and efficiently. When discipline departs, the machine breaks down.

The test of discipline is when you err. The bungled shot, the fly-away shot, are invitations to disaster on the golf course. The undisciplined player panics or loses his composure. Dismay gives way to anger and anger to despair while his wild shots carom off the trees. And he carries the searing memory of his experience through the next two or three holes which, in turn, become disorderly routs.

The disciplined golfer pushes the mistake out of his mind immediately and goes methodically about restoring the pattern of his game. He retains control of his game, resumes play and, by a fine chip or a putt, erases the deficit caused by the bad shot—and, at the same time, unnerves his opponent.

I had this business of positive thinking hammered home in a conversation with Arnold Palmer back in 1960, at a time when I was struggling across my own private slough of despond. It was after the Mobile Open (which Palmer had won) and he and I were overnight guests aboard a yacht prior to flying to West Palm Beach in the morning for the next stop on the circuit.

We were lying in our bunks, waiting for the sandman to check us in, and I congratulated Arnold on a great year which had included victories in the Masters and the Open championships. I suggested that he had accomplished something fantastic in winning the way he had won, with Frank Merriwell finishes.

"I never thought of it like that," said Palmer drowsily. "I just kind of see what it is I have to do, and I just make up my mind that I'm going to do it. If I have a long putt to make, I just think about making that putt. I just shut all thought of missing it out of mind . . ."

It gave me something to chew on before I fell asleep. I wasn't too sure whether he had said something very important, or hadn't said anything at all. But the longer I turned over his comments in my mind the more firmly convinced I became that Arnie had stated one of the eternal verities of golf. Winning is a state of mind.

8

"...It's how you play the game."

The Gentleman's Game

No game in the annals of sport is as rich in tradition and folklore as golf. None appeals more strongly to the essentially decent instincts of the human animal. Golf goes far beyond its simplest definition as a form of recreation. It is almost a way of life for many, a sort of testing ground for the cultivated virtues and a mirror which reflects a more gracious pattern of civilization.

From its earliest beginning, golf has been a gentleman's game—to be played as much for the sake of the game as for the contest. Its rules of conduct were drafted by gentlemen, not to be *imposed* on the player, but rather to be *adopted* by him. There is a subtle but very significant difference here, and it goes to the very heart of the game.

No other sporting game that comes readily to mind is played without judge, umpire or referee. True, in tournament golf we do have such officials, but the position is almost honorary. Rarely does the player have occasion to call for a ruling, and even more rarely is he penalized for an abridgment of the rules. The game is, essentially, a contest between the player and the golf course, and the player is expected to observe the rules and to play the course as he finds it.

The competition among the players arises out of a matching of their scores. The contest is strictly between the players and the course. Here is an important distinction. A clear understanding of this marks the difference between a golfer and a slob. The sorriest spectacle on a golf course is to watch the steady erosion of the rules by four slobs who are frustrated by the course and connive to conquer it by chicanery.

I was impressed on my first visit to St. Andrews, the spiritual home of the game, by the scrupulous respect the ordinary players—the townspeople—had for the course. It's almost an article of faith with these people to touch the ball only twice in the play of a hole: when they set it on the tee, and again when they pick it out of the cup. You won't find a St. Andrean poking the ball up on a tuft of grass to improve his lie, or conceding himself a free lift from behind a whin bush, or stretching the rules to drop in the clear four- or five-club lengths from an obstruction.

By no means do I mean to imply that golf is found in its purest form only at St. Andrews. Rather, it was a case of coming away from that shrine with a strengthened sense of respect for the traditions of the game, and a sharpened sense of responsibility to preserve them. I've observed the same scrupulous adherence to the written rules and the unwritten code of conduct wherever gentlemen gather to play the finest game in the world.

I've led you deliberately into this discussion because I don't believe it's enough just to master the mechanics of hitting a golf ball. You could become the finest shot-maker who ever stepped on a tee, and still have no place on a golf course. Unless you're aware of your responsibilities to yourself, to your playing partners, to the course and to the game of golf, your education as a golfer is incomplete.

It's interesting to observe that, where golf is incorporated into the physical education curriculum of a college, invariably instruction begins in the classroom with attention to golf course etiquette and the rules of the game. I know one state university where students enrolling for the golf class are required to pass a written test on both subjects before they are permitted to swing a club and step onto the golf course. I'm sure this is true of most other schools, and I heartily endorse the method.

Let's review some of the common "rules of the road" on the course.

As we remarked at the outset of this chapter, golf is a gentleman's game. Its players are expected to observe the natural laws of courtesy and consideration for the rights of others. The first of nine cardinal rules of etiquette spelled out by the United States Golf Association is a reminder that you should never intrude upon the concentration of another. Never move about or talk when he is addressing the ball or playing a shot. Don't stand too close to him, or directly behind the ball in such a position that your presence will serve to distract him. And, of course, you should never volunteer advice at a time like this—or, for that matter, any other time unless it relates to playing conditions that could influence the other's strategy of play.

Don't hold up other players needlessly, including others in your own foursome. When you have the honor on the tee, be prepared to set up your ball and hit it. This is not the time to run the ball through the washer and engage in idle conversation—especially if the course is crowded and another foursome is pressing you.

Similarly, through the green, move along with a minimum of delay. This means studying your shot as you approach the ball and deciding promptly which club to use. If your ball goes astray and you anticipate a delay while you search, by all means wave the following players through. Or, if the course is opening up ahead of you while a foursome is pressing along behind yours, regard this as a signal that you and your group are becoming a bottleneck. Again, be a good fellow and permit the following foursome to play through. Don't be a fairway squatter. Nothing can ruin the other fellow's outing and wreck his game like stop-and-go golf—shifting impatiently from one foot to the other all afternoon, hole after hole, while some louts up ahead criss-cross the fairway in an endless slow-motion parade. It's probably happened to you more than once. Don't be responsible for it happening to somebody else.

And don't die on the green. Line up your putts quickly and run them in without a lot of unnecessary surveying and circling. I don't suggest you hurry your putts, but putting in recent years has become almost an absurd ballet, with more pacing back and forth than you'll find in an old-fashioned quadrille. Take a practice swing if you must, but try to limit it to one. I don't know why it is, but thousands and thousands of golfers seem to share a conviction that they have to take three practice swings before they can move up to a putt and hit it. Why three, I don't know. Maybe it has some obscure religious significance. If so, I would suggest that the putting surface is not the proper place for such rites. A simple silent prayer on the first tee should do nicely.

Traditionally, the player farthest from the hole takes precedence in the putting order. In formal play this could remain a standard pattern (although I don't know why). However, in friendly and informal games, in the interest of speeding up play, I see no reason why a player near the cup shouldn't hole out and remove himself from the traffic pattern. Again, it is simply a question of consideration for the other fellow, particularly if another foursome is on your heels.

When the last person has holed his putt, replace the flagstick and move off the green immediately. This is not the place to hold a caucus while you tabulate your scores. The arithmetic can be done en route to the next tee.

We have concerned ourselves only with those pressing behind us, and with the need to play forward without need-less delay. Let's flip the coin and examine the other face—when you are a member of the following foursome. Here again, however irked you may become, you have an obliga-

tion to practice courtesy. Try not to steam up your glasses.
Above all, never hit while the players up ahead are still
within range. Not only is this a gross breach of etiquette,
but you could cause personal injury and wind up playing in
a legal tournament with lawyers and insurance adjusters.

Your concern for the welfare of your fellow man should
be matched by a concern for the course. Even when you're
a club member, you are still a guest of the greenskeeper on
the course. Remember that. You have a moral obligation to
leave the course as you found it, just as you would have the
same obligation to leave someone's home as you found it
after you'd been a house guest. Clean up behind you and
repair any damage you may have caused. This means raking
over and smoothing out tracks and explosion craters when
you leave a sand bunker. Again, think of the fellow playing
behind you.

On the green, protect and preserve the putting surface.
If you're traveling by golf cart, abandon it well away from
the green and complete the journey on foot. The walk will
do you good. And be careful handling the flagstick. When
you remove it from the cup, take pains not to wrench the
cup itself out of its bed, nor fling the stick carelessly on the
putting surface, gouging it.

If a caddie is tending the stick, he should be trained to
handle it properly without damaging the putting surface. If
his training has been faulty, make it your responsibility to
school him.

Repair ball marks on the green and replace divots taken
on the fairway. Most golfers are considerate about performing the first chore, but too many are lazy and indifferent
about replacing their divots. This is one of the tests of golf
as a gentleman's game. Nobody is going to spring out of the
underbrush and compel you to repair your divot marks.
This is a simple matter of self-discipline, a case of being
sensitive to the rights of others and developing a habit of
thoughtfulness. It pays off in character-building.

There is an established order of precedence on the
course. Foursomes and threesomes have right-of-way and

other matches should defer to them as a matter of accepted golf course courtesy. Singles have no standing whatever. Similarly, any match going the full eighteen-hole route has priority on the course over those playing a shorter distance.

Under no circumstances should you practice on any fairway or green in use. Under some conditions (for instance, late in the day, when there is no traffic on the course), you may, with the approval of the professional, use a section of fairway for a limited time and for a special reason. Or you may practice trap shots from a playing bunker, again when it's not in normal use.

But never practice putting on a playing green. I have yet to encounter a golf course that lacked a practice putting green. Use it. Give the playing greens every chance to recuperate from the heavy traffic of the day.

On the course, you never play more than one ball at a time. Even if you're the only person on the course, it's still a bad practice—for the simple reason that it isn't even good practice! All you're doing is hitting twice as many shots as you would in the normal course of play. And, if that's all you want, go find a driving range and knock your brains out.

The only exception is when you play a provisional ball, under the rules, for one believed lost or out of bounds. Otherwise, playing a second ball is an outrageous breach of golf course etiquette.

At all times, remember that golf is a game and a golf course is a place of scenic charm and tranquility. Enjoy them both for what they have to offer: light exercise, mental relaxation and good fellowship in pleasant surroundings. In a world full of tumult and shouting, this is something worth preserving. You can do your share.

The Rules of Golf

Golf is like solitaire. When you cheat, you cheat only yourself. It's the one game where you are frequently in the curious position of policing yourself. Nobody but you will

ever know that the ball moved as you were addressing it, or
that you tamped down the tall grass to improve your lie, or
rooted out an intrusive weed. If you don't call the penalty,
nobody else will—and you'll be the loser for it.

There is an honor code that governs the game of golf,
handed along to us by generations of golfers. Alan Robertson,
club-maker at St. Andrews more than a hundred years ago,
is said to have lost a match at Musselburgh involving a sub-
stantial purse when he called a penalty on himself for
inadvertently flicking a ridge of sand as he addressed the
ball in a bunker. Nobody perceived it but he. Coming down
to more recent times, the immortal Bob Jones called a penalty on himself when the ball moved as he soled his club at
the address. It cost him an Open championship.

This is why I say the rules are drafted for *adoption* by
golfers, not to be *imposed* upon them. You, as a player, are
expected to tabulate your own shots. You are expected, as
one who subscribes to the honor code of the game, to observe
the rules in their entirety and to assess your own penalties
when you abridge them. In turn, you have a right to expect
your playing partners and opponents to do the same. Without rules, there is no game—and without self-enforcement,
there are no rules.

But the Rules of Golf are more than just a catalog of
penalties. They also work to save you strokes, and for this
reason they deserve your earnest study. Arnold Palmer won
his first Masters' championship in 1958 by knowing his
rights under the rules. Under a local rule, he knew he was
entitled to a free lift of an embedded ball. He asked for the
ruling, was granted his free lift, which saved him two strokes,
and won the tournament by one stroke!

Always remember that you may lift a ball without
penalty from casual water—even in a sand trap. Of course,
in this case, you have to drop the ball elsewhere in the trap
or, if you prefer, drop outside the bunker and take a one-
stroke penalty.

I can remember another incident at Palm Springs, this

time on the 18th hole at Bermuda Dunes. I hit a slight fade which caught the side of a slope and kicked off into the water of a pond. Thinking the water was a lateral hazard, I dug out my rule book and read about two-thirds of the rule on this situation—to the effect that I could drop out not more than two club lengths from the point of entry.

If I had read further, I would have learned that I could drop out two club lengths, but I would have to keep the point where the ball entered the hazard between me and the hole. I wedged the ball up to the green, then decided to ask for an official ruling. It's a good thing I didn't hole out. After talking with the official, I had to go back and drop out of the hazard again—this time, on the other side of the lake!

Now I stuck a 6-iron shot about a good foot from the pin and dropped the putt. So I was down in 3, but took three penalty strokes for a six—one to drop out of the pond and two for hitting a shot illegally.

You are the sole judge of an unplayable lie. You may elect to drop the ball in playable position within two club lengths on either side of the unplayable lie at a cost of a penalty stroke. Or you may drop any place back of the unplayable position—all the way back to the tee, if you like.

Incidentally, there is no penalty for playing the wrong ball out of a hazard if you then play your own ball because, under the rules, you cannot move the ball to identify it. Otherwise, a player playing the wrong ball is punished by the loss of the hole at match play, or by two strokes at medal play.

You are entitled to lift a ball without penalty and drop it not more than two club lengths in any direction (but not nearer the hole) if your line of play is obstructed by a shelter, building, hoses, piece of maintenance equipment, bench, tin can, paper, etc. Or, if any obstruction is movable, it may be removed from your line. Fixed obstructions which are part of the course, such as boundary stakes, walls and fences, paths and roads, do not fall in this category. You have to deal with these things as you find them.

On the green, any ball mark may be repaired at any time. This includes tamping the repaired spot with your foot. A ball poised on the lip of the cup is allowed only a few seconds to fall. After that, it is considered to have come to rest and, if it is your opponent's, you have a right to knock it away, conceding him his next putt.

A provisional ball may be played for one which may be lost or out of bounds, but not for a ball that may be unplayable or in a water hazard. If you hit a provisional ball, you may play it until you reach the original ball.

By all means, carry a copy of the Rules of Golf with you at all times and consult it whenever you are in doubt. You should familiarize yourself with the rules, not with the idea of becoming a clubhouse lawyer—there are enough of those in the game!—but rather as a form of stroke insurance and because golf is a game of rules. Knowing them and adhering to them makes it a better game.

Become acquainted with the local rules, particularly when you are playing as a guest at a strange club. Usually, these are printed on your score card. Study them before you tee off. Ignorance of the rules, like ignorance of the law, is no excuse.

Essentially, the rules of the game fall into three broad categories and are based on three fundamental principles:

1. You play the ball as it lies.
2. You play the course as you find it.
   and
3. Where neither principle applies, let the rule of fair play settle the issue.

Somewhere in the fifty-seven pages of rules published by the U.S.G.A. you will find a rule that covers virtually every conceivable situation that can arise on the course, and every player owes it to himself and his playing partners to be familiar with the rules. Although the rules makers have tried to anticipate every eventuality, there isn't a year passes which doesn't produce its quota of bizarre circumstances.

Here, the third principle is applied and the case usually referred for judgment to the U.S.G.A. as the court of last appeal.

However, in the normal course of events, the average golfer can expect to play a lifetime of golf without encountering any problem that can't be resolved by direct reference to the rule book. The important thing is to have a reasonably good knowledge of the rules and a genuine respect for them. They deserve your respect because, aside from the Canon Law of the Roman Catholic Church, they probably represent the only authentic body of international law that exists. If you hit the flagstick from any place on the green, or within 20 feet of the pin, it's going to cost you a two-stroke penalty whether you're in St. Andrews, Scotland, or St. Louis, Missouri.

So, by all means, play by the rules. It makes a better game of it—and makes you a better person for it.

You're on the Tee

Golf is the game of a lifetime. There's room on the course for toddlers and oldsters of both sexes, for the par shooter and the 100 shooter. There's nothing else quite like it in the realm of sport. It combines the zest of competition with the easy cameraderie of fellowship and, if taken according to the prescription, is a grand form of recreation.

It's only human nature to strive for improvement and I can only hope that this little volume whittles a few strokes off your handicap. But don't become so concerned with your scoring that you spoil the game for yourself. We pros are the only ones who really have to sweat this game out because those figures that go down on the card determine what kind of lives our families will enjoy, what kind of schools the kids will attend and what kind of a neighborhood they'll call home.

Most of us touring professionals wouldn't change places with you people behind the ropes, but that doesn't mean we don't know moments when we envy you your amiable

Saturday game. For us, the cruel economics of the daily grind rubs some of the glitter off the game. We envy you your freedom to enjoy it as a recreation.

By all means, play the game to the very best of your ability. Work at it, because the rewards, measured in self-satisfaction, are worth it. But play it for enjoyment, for the companionship that your weekend foursome offers, and for the light exercise you derive from it. Don't take your bad shots home with you and don't let the game become a demon that obsesses you.

It's a fun game. So, have fun . . .